Winter Trails: Maine

"Marty Basch has unlocked one of the great secrets of the Maine woods: They're as fun to explore in the winter as they are in the summer, maybe even more so. And he makes it easy for anyone who wants to follow his tracks into the snow."

—Andrew Vietze, Registered Maine Guide

Help Us Keep This Guide Up to Date

Every effort has been made by the author and editors to make this guide as accurate and useful as possible. However, many things can change after a guide is published—establishments close, phone numbers change, trails are rerouted, facilities come under new management, etc.

We would love to hear from you concerning your experiences with this guide and how you feel it could be improved and kept up to date. While we may not be able to respond to all comments and suggestions, we'll take them to heart and we'll make certain to share them with the author. Please send your comments and suggestions to the following address:

The Globe Pequot Press
Reader Response/Editorial Department
P.O. Box 480
Guilford, CT 06437

Or you may e-mail us at

editorial@globe-pequot.com

Thanks for your input, and happy travels!

winter trails™

Maine

The Best Cross-Country Ski & Snowshoe Trails

by
MARTY BASCH

The Globe Pequot Press

GUILFORD, CONNECTICUT

Winter Trails is a trademark of The Globe Pequot Press.

Cover photographs: © Brian Bailey/Adventure Photo & Film; inset photo © Andy Anderson/Adventure Photo & Film
Cover and interior design: Nancy Freeborn
Trail maps created by Equator Graphics © The Globe Pequot Press
State map: Lisa Reneson
Photo credits: pages xx, 73, and 104, courtesy of Maine Nordic Ski Council; all other photos courtesy of the author.

Library of Congress Cataloging-in-Publication Data

Basch, Marty.
   Winter trails: Maine : the best cross-country ski & snowshoe trails / Marty Basch. — 1st ed.
      p.   cm. — (Winter trails series)
   Includes bibliographical references (p.).
   ISBN 0-7627-0556-6
      1. Cross-country skiing—Maine Guidebooks.   2. Snowshoes and snowshoeing—Maine Guidebooks.   3. Cross-country ski trails—Maine Guidebooks. I. Title.   II. Series.
   GV854.5.M2B37   1999
   917.4104'43—dc21   99-37535
                                                            CIP

Manufactured in the United States of America
First Edition/First Printing

Also by Marty Basch

Winter Trails Vermont & New Hampshire
The White Mountain Ride Guide
Above the Circle
Against the Wind

To my parents,

Lynn and Mitch Basch,

on forty years of togetherness.

Maine

Contents

m a i n e

Acknowledgments

Maine is so vast, that it is nearly impossible for one person to come up with a collection of "best" trails without tapping into the knowledge and experience of those who love the state's winter pathways.

Thanks go out to Steve Finch, Carla Marcus, Wende Gray, Nancy Marshall, Charlene Williams, Heidi Davidson, Steve Jackson, Mike Wheeler, Sue Foster, Rob Tice, Jeff Foltz, Steve Swenson, Sally Swenson, Jeff Welt, Mike Gallagher, Susan Benson, Karen Francoeur, Don Nodine, Bee Lavasseur, Bob LeRoy, Arlene Hadley-LeRoy, Matt and Wendy Polstein, Judy Kellogg Markowsky, Rod Newton, Fritz Appleby, Pete Goheen, Steve Higgins, Carl Theriault, Mike Voisine, Bruce Farnham, and Susan Richardson for sharing their resources, time, and expertise (and even a few favorite trails). Ryan Cota gets a special thanks for his fast-flying company across Moosehead Lake and up Mount Kineo.

On the editorial side of things, the people at Globe Pequot Press have been a pleasure to work with. One thousand words of thanks to Laura Strom. Kudos to Dan Spinella and Shelley Wolf for attention to details.

A special thanks goes to Jan Duprey, who always made room for love in those insulated bags packed with goodies for the road.

Introduction

Welcome to winter in Maine!

Miles and miles of trails wind through the snow-encrusted forests, mountains, and valleys of the Pine Tree State. Nature centers, state parks, national forests, community recreation areas, downhill and cross-country ski areas, open fields, and your own backyards all provide access to winter trails.

Trails that take summer's hikers to the summit of a 4,000 footer or meander gently around a pond reflecting in the autumn sun become paths to play for cross-country skiers and snowshoers.

Those who love winter know the silence of a solitary forest trek. They see the beauty of a snowfall in a pine-laden forest. They know that the bugs are gone, and there are fewer people. The cold doesn't bother them. Instead, it becomes a challenge unto itself.

Those who love winter also know about the dangers that lurk around the bend. Changing weather, sudden squalls, flimsy ice, and more can turn a nice day into a race against death.

For those who prefer human-powered transportation, winter is a time for cross-country skiing and snowshoeing. Each mode of travel has its own benefits. If you can walk, you can snowshoe. If you can walk, you can cross-country ski too, but it might take considerably more effort. Nonetheless, winter can be an enjoyable experience.

Maine is home to a great number of winter trails. The outings in this book include trips from the White Mountain National Forest to Acadia National Park, from Baxter State Park to the far reaches of Fort Kent. There are also excursions through state parks, conservancy lands, and cross-country ski areas. Most of the outings do not have a fee, though trail passes are needed at the cross-country ski areas. In 1996, the White Mountain National Forest instituted a program that requires users to purchase a recreation pass to park at trailheads within the forest boundaries.

Skiers and snowshoers aren't the only recreationists using the winter trails. You'll also encounter hikers and snowmobiles on certain outings. Only a few trails that are used by snowmobiles are covered in this book. But snowmobilers still use these trails, and groom some of them too.

Each outing is rated for difficulty, includes directions for driving to the trailheads and for getting around the trails, provides the distance of each journey, offers suggestions for last minute grocery shopping and posttrip

The view by the bridge at Big Lyford Pond near Greenville is serene, with tall pines and a chilly, flowing stream. It's scenery such as this that makes a winter trek in Maine so worthwhile.

meals, and comes with helpful phone numbers. The trips can take a full day or just a couple of hours.

Whichever way you get around the trails of winter, be sure to be smart and enjoy.

Equipment

Technology marches on. If you have been paying any attention to what you strap to your feet, you'll know that snowshoe and cross-country ski equipment have made a bit of a leap since their early users, like the Eskimos and Vikings, romped through the woods and across the tundra.

Don't fret. The old stuff still works. Those wooden ash snowshoes over the fireplace, in the attic, or on the wall of the garage will still do the trick. So will those three-pin skinny skis you bought at a yard sale on a whim a decade or so ago.

Wooden snowshoes with the basic bear paw design are still being made, but the shape of the snowshoe has changed, it has been streamlined. There is more choice as far as bindings go, and the snowshoe is lightweight. Some modern day snowshoes also come with crampons affixed.

If you are new to the sport and not sure if you are going to like it, the best bet is to rent a pair, either at a sporting goods store or cross-country ski center. Don't be afraid to pepper the staff with questions—that's what they are there for.

How do you choose the right snowshoe for you? There is a three-step process, based on snow conditions, terrain, body weight, and price.

The first thing to do is figure out what kind of snowshoeing you plan to do. Most activity falls into either the recreational or mountaineering category. Recreational snowshoeing revolves around family outings, walking, running, hiking, aerobic cross-training, and day treks. These are activities usually done on easy, broken trails.

Mountaineering centers around wilderness excursions, overnight adventures, and climbing approaches and steep terrain. These outings are usually done in varying conditions, from deep powder to unbroken trails to windswept snow.

Next, figure out your total body weight. That's not just how much you weigh, but the weight of the total package—body, clothing, and anticipated weight of backpacks.

The last step is to make comparisons. Based on how you expect to use your shoes, take a look around at the store. Ask about prices. Sample the various bindings to figure out which one will work best for you. Remember, the outdoors in winter will be a lot colder than a retail store. Make sure the bindings are easy to use.

Some snowshoers use ski poles while on a trek. They help with and are useful during ascents and descents. Lean on them if a tree isn't available.

Choosing the right cross-country ski equipment is a bit more complicated because you must purchase skis, boots, bindings, and poles. Basically, you can choose from the waxable or waxless skis that are used for recreational or

Skis stand at attention, ready to glide.

backcountry skiing. Of course groups have subcategories, which are based on weight, ability, style, and terrain. Nordic skiers also must decide if they want a ski for skating or the classic skiing technique.

If you just want to get out and back on easy terrain at your local park or cross-country ski center, stick to the waxless skis. They perform well under most conditions and give you one less thing to worry about.

Racers and more experienced skiers like waxable skis. They can get more glide out of the ski, which usually means a bit less work. But you must learn the right way to wax them, based on temperature and snow conditions.

As for what type of ski to get, as was the case with snowshoeing, figure out what kind of skiing you want to do. Those skiers who like groomed and tracked trails stick to recreational skis, while those who prefer more untamed conditions gravitate to wider, stronger-edged skis.

Proper Clothing

Are you wondering what to wear when heading outside to snowshoe or cross-country ski? Just remember one word—layers. Even though it could be downright cold outside, get ready to be quite warm while you are engaged in activity. You'll cool off quickly when you stop. To dress for comfort, choose lightweight and breathable underwear as the first layer. On top of those, have a layer that acts as an absorbent, like a sweater or fleece. The outside layer should be a wind-resistant shell.

The idea behind dressing this way is to better manage your body's temperature while snowshoeing or skiing. Layering gives you greater control than one thick layer of insulation, like a parka. By putting on and taking off layers, you act like a thermostat, regulating the body's temperature. As you exert more energy, your body will start to heat up. When that happens, remove a layer. Cold? Put the layers back on.

The first layer is responsible for your skin. Perspiration is no fun in winter. That's why it's best to stay away from cotton and consider a layer that wicks away wetness from the skin and traps a blanket of dry, warm air. The middle layer has a couple of jobs: One is to encourage the perspiration to get on out of there; the other is to insulate by trapping warm air. Materials like fleece or wool are able to continue insulating even when wet.

The same principles apply to pants. In general, your legs don't need as much insulation as your upper body. Still, the layer next to your skin should be just like the torso layer. On extremely cold, windy, or rainy days, you should use a shell on top of the insulating layer.

A hat is of primary importance. An uncovered head is a source of heat loss. Cover it to stay warm and dry. Take your hat off to cool down.

Gloves and mittens are also part of the proper clothing arsenal. You should wear fleece, wool, or insulated gloves. A fleece glove with a shell is excellent on extreme weather days. The choice between gloves or mittens is a personal one.

Dry and warm feet are happy feet. Happy feet are essential to an outdoor winter experience. Forget cotton. Fleece and wool are the mantra. Some people like two layers of socks, one thin and the other thick. Again, this is a personal choice.

Cross-country skiers have a couple of choices for their boots. For the most part low-cut boots are better for groomed trails. Higher boots that go above the ankle provide better support and are usually associated with deeper, ungroomed snow conditions.

Waterproof hiking boots with decent ankle support should prove well suited to snowshoeing. Plastic mountaineering boots can also be used for extended trips. For those casual outings, you can wear almost anything. But the idea is to stay warm and dry, so any rubber, insulated, or hiking boot will suffice.

A few accessories are helpful during an outdoor winter excursion. A neck warmer is an excellent choice. Not only will it keep your neck warm, it can double as a goofy-looking hat, wearable in the solitude of the woods. The neck warmer can also triple as a headband if it is folded in half. A headband keeps ears warm on those sunny winter days called spring! Gaiters are a good idea—they keep the snow from getting in between your boots and socks.

Use sunglasses to minimize squinting. Wear goggles on extreme days to protect eyes from the wind and cold. If vanity is a concern, always carry a baseball cap to ward off "hathead."

Consider a camera or binoculars for capturing those wonderful human and wildlife moments.

Safety

In winter, trail conditions can vary drastically from day to day. Plan ahead. Winter in Maine can be unpredictable and severe. Changing weather, dropping temperatures, shorter days, and deep snow are all challenges while you are out on skis and snowshoes. Breaking trail can be an exhaustive experience. If an excursion takes you to higher elevations over open rock faces and above the tree line, snowshoes with crampons are necessary. Taking extra warm clothing and a few safety items is imperative. Winter is rather harsh on mistakes. Though what you carry in a backpack or fanny pack is a personal choice, some suggested items include a guidebook, map, compass, insulated water bottles, high-energy foods, waterproof matches, flashlight with spare batteries (kept warm), rope, duct tape, toilet paper, and ski wax.

A first-aid kit is also recommended. It can include items like pain relief medicine, adhesive bandages, gauze, ace bandages, and antiseptic.

Hypothermia and frostbite are two dangerous threats in winter. Hypothermia, considered the leading cause of backcountry emergencies, occurs when the body's core temperature drops below normal. The most serious result of hypothermia is that it impairs judgment. Symptoms include shivering, disorientation, loss of coordination, and slurred speech. In order to prevent hypothermia, wear clothing that keeps you well insulated. Be sure to stay dry. Hydrate. Drink more than you think you need. Keep an eye on the weather. Be cognizant of the conditions of people you are traveling with.

Frostbite occurs when tissue is damaged by severe cold and wind. Pale skin and numbness are its two basic symptoms, though as the condition worsens, the affected area can freeze. As with hypothermia, frostbite can be prevented by wearing proper clothing that provides warmth and allows for flowing circulation. Eat and hydrate well, too.

Even in the cold of winter, drinking plenty of fluids is necessary to properly hydrate your body. When tired, take breaks, especially if a bench is handy.

Before heading out, always plan ahead. Allow a conservative three miles per hour for a cross-country experience and one mile per hour for snowshoeing. Remember, there is safety in numbers. If you are inexperienced, don't head out alone. Take into consideration the abilities of those in your group, the weather, terrain, and hours of light left in the day. Many outdoor clubs, organizations, schools, and community centers offer first aid and outside skill courses and workshops. Take one.

Above all, use common sense.

Navigation

It's relatively easy to get lost on a trail in winter. All you have to do is not pay attention and a pleasant day snowshoeing up the side of a 4,000-foot mountain can turn into a race against daylight and disaster. Though beautiful, the whiteness of winter is also deceiving because it blankets landmarks that may be familiar to summer hikers and walkers. Soft and airy snowflakes can cover a stream, turning one misstep into a plunge into wetness. Stray just a few inches off the main trail, and you can find yourself thigh-deep in a cold, hard, snowy trap.

In general, snowshoeing or cross-country skiing at a groomed, fee ski center is easy. There are maps available to you before you head out and the trails are usually well signed, with arrows pointing the way. Many centers also have maps along the route, especially at junctions, which indicate where you are within the network. To alleviate any concerns, it is always best to question the frontline warrior behind the desk in the center's office for the latest information. These experienced outdoorspeople can even outline the route with a transparent marker to allay your fears. Cross-country ski networks are patrolled as well; these patrols look for skiers and shoers on the trails before the system shuts down for the day.

To avoid any confusion, always stick to the trail.

Follow blazes and signs, such as this sign for the International Appalachian Trail, and be sure to stick to the trail.

In the woods and forests, blazes are the key to successful navigation. Trees are marked at varying intervals with different colored paint. If you follow the blazes, you are following the trail. Signs also mark the way. But in winter the snow can either cover or obscure a blaze. Severe storms can throw blowdowns in the path, which can be confusing. During periods of soft light and deep snow, white blazes or markings only 4 feet above the ground can be hard to spot.

Of course, following other people's tracks makes navigation easy. But if you are trailblazing in unfamiliar terrain, the task increases in difficulty. Always look for blazes. Consider trips that go out and back. That way, you can follow your tracks back.

Carry a map and a compass. Know how to use them.

The Maine State Police can offer assistance during emergencies. There are toll-free numbers available statewide. In Augusta, call (800) 452–4664; in Gray, call (800) 482–0730; in Houlton, call (800) 924–2261; in Orono, call (800) 432–7381; in Skowhegan, call (800) 452–4664; and in Thomaston, call (800) 339–0819. For cellular phones, the statewide emergency number is *77.

Courtesy

Snowshoeing has boomed in popularity. With popularity, comes the responsibility to learn trail courtesy and etiquette. Snowshoeing in deep snow is fun, but many like the groomed, compacted trails at a cross-country ski area. There are some areas that forbid snowshoeing on the groomed trails, instead providing snowshoers with trails all their own. However, snowshoers and skiers do share many trails—both in fee areas and in the woods.

Give skiers the right of way. Skiers are generally going faster than snowshoers. Plus, it's easier and quicker to get around on snowshoes.

Don't snowshoe on ski tracks. The beauty of the snowshoe is that it can go virtually anywhere. If you are snowshoeing on a skating lane, stay to the right. If possible, stick to the edge of the trail and on the deeper snow. Skiing on tracks marred by snowshoe prints is nervewracking.

Follow the rules. If at a ski center, stick to the rules. If in the woods, and a trail is "for skiers only," pay attention to it.

Dogs and the outdoors can be quite controversial. Lovable Fido with his warming wad of fur is comforting in the cold of winter. But not everyone is a dog lover. Canines leave behind all sorts of indicators of their presence, from imprints on the trails to poop. And humans don't always use common sense when it comes to pets. What is a a pleasure to one person, can be quite aggravating to another.

There are a few cross-country ski centers affiliated with the Maine Nordic Ski Council that allow dogs on the trails. According to the council, Harris Farm in Dayton welcomes

Many skiers like to take Fido out on the trails. Not every touring center in Maine allows pets on the trails. Some do, others don't.

dogs on all trails midweek. Leave them home on the weekends. If you want, Harris Farm will even supply you with a poop scoop. It's for your dog.

Five Fields Farm in Bridgton and Carter's Cross-Country Ski Centers in Oxford and Bethel allow dogs on the trails any day. The Sunday River Cross-Country Center in Bethel allows dogs on the ½-mile Farm Loop Trail, while the Narrow Gauge Trail at the Sugarloaf Outdoor Center is open to dogs. The Birches Resort in Rockwood and Little Lyford Pond Camps and Lodge near Greenville also allow dogs.

Should you bring your dog, act responsibly. That means you, too.

Trail Classification

The outings in the Winter Trails series are based on a three-tier classification system—easiest, more difficult, most difficult. There aren't any hard-and-fast rules for determining the level of difficulty. In general, an outing rated *easiest* is one that has flat and gentle terrain. It can be done in a couple of hours. A *more difficult* excursion has more rolling terrain. You'll need better technique to conquer the hills. The distance is a bit longer than on an easy trip. A *most difficult* outing has the most challenging terrain, requires advanced skill levels, and can be long and/or remote. Elevation can also play a factor.

Please note: A trail that might be easiest on snowshoes is not always easiest on skis. Heading down or up a particular section of a trail on snowshoes is a far different experience than on skis. Consider your outings accordingly.

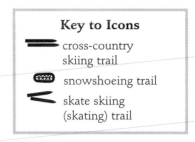

maine

Peary Mountain
Brownfield, Maine

Type of trail: ⬤ ▬

Also used by Snowmobilers, hikers

Distance: 2.0 miles round-trip

Terrain: Gentle ascent up a small mountain, with commanding western Maine vistas

Trail difficulty: Easiest snowshoe, more difficult ski

Surface quality: Packed by snowmobiles

Time: 2 hours

Food and facilities: There is no water or rest rooms available on this excursion. For groceries, Fryeburg has what's needed. Emery's (207–935–2864) on Portland Street is a full-service grocery store. Across the street is the Fryeburg House of Pizza (207–935–4172). For lodging try the Admiral Peary House Bed and Breakfast, 9 Elm Street, Fryeburg (207–935–3365). Peary lived there. They rent snowshoes at the B&B and have snowshoe trails. Many overnight opportunities exist over the border in North Conway, New Hampshire.

Phone numbers: For information call the Maine Publicity Bureau (207–623–0363).

From the open ledges of this small Brownfield mountain, you'll have views of the White Mountains of New Hampshire and the peaks and hills of western Maine. At about 2.0 miles round-trip, a snowshoe trip up to the south summit of Peary Mountain is a relatively easy excursion. This is a good warm-up before tackling more difficult peaks. For skiers

the packed snowmobile trail makes for a gradual ascent and a winding downhill.

The mountain bears the name of one of Maine's most famous explorers—Rear Admiral Robert E. Peary. Peary, who grew up in Maine, is credited

From the top of Peary Mountain, snowshoers can look into neighboring New Hampshire while enjoying the vistas Maine has to offer as well.

with discovering the North Pole in April 1909. He lived with his widowed mother in Fryeburg for two years on graduating from Bowdoin College in 1877. The woods and mountains called to Peary, and he answered by becoming an accomplished taxidermist and civil engineer. He loved to explore the White Mountains and often hiked to the top of little Jockey Cap in Fryeburg, where a bronze profile of the outlying peaks stands as a monument to Peary. Jockey Cap, located 1.0 mile east of Fryeburg on Route 302, is a short 0.2-mile snowshoe to a ledge with panoramic views.

While living in Fryeburg, Peary worked as the town surveyor and justice of the peace. One day he noticed an ad in the post office calling for government draftsmen. Peary applied and won the Washington, D.C. appointment along with three others. He left Fryeberg and a career was born.

Directions at a glance

0.0 Pick up snowmobile trail on Farnsworth Road near wooden bridge that spans Little Saco River. Travel south on unmarked snowmobile trail, watching for occasional snowmobile signs.

0.8 Make a hard left by stone wall and head 0.2 mile to south summit.

1.0 Return via same route.

Peary Mountain is only 958 feet high, but it serves up vistas to rival some of the big peaks. There are two peaks, but only a trail to the south cone. It is possible to bushwhack to the main summit.

The unmarked snowmobile trail that leads to the top of the south summit leaves Farnsworth Road near a wooden bridge that spans the Little Saco River. The trail is not blazed with paint markings on trees, but it is identified with occasional snowmobile signs.

Initially, the trail is level. About a quarter-mile into it, there is a dip, which indicates the start of the gradual ascent to a saddle with a clearing. A small stream flows along the trail near the 0.5-mile mark. Wind-ravaged birches bend by the trailside as you gain elevation. The trees are reminders of a January 1998 ice storm that devastated particular regions of Maine and neighboring New Hampshire.

The trail is wide enough for snowshoers to travel two abreast. It approaches the low point between the two peaks at a small clearing that houses the remnants of an old dwelling, a stone wall, two stone benches, and a stone fireplace. The stone cellar invites cautious exploration, while the benches are a welcome resting spot. The views lay ahead.

It is here skiers should change over to snowshoes or winter hiking boots. The north cone is reachable with a 0.4-mile bushwhack to the right.

However, the south summit calls. Follow the stone wall to the left and ascend to the bare, open ledges of Peary's southern top. Deep snow will make the short, steep ascent easier. Windswept snow or ice invites caution.

A stone bench shares the summit with scrub trees and granite ledges. Walk around for the changing views. The main summit of Peary Mountain is due north. Beyond that peak are New Hampshire's White Mountains, with landmarks like the fire tower atop Kearsarge Mountain, Mount Washington, and Mount Chocorua. Peer at some of western Maine's natural features, Lovewell Pond and Pleasant Mountain. Look down into tiny Fryeburg and Brownfield.

Retrace your snowshoe tracks back to the junction, then snake down the trail, following the legendary footsteps of Peary, whose spirit still resides in the mountains of Maine.

How to get there

From Fryeburg, travel south on Routes 113/5 5.0 miles to Farnsworth Road. Turn right on Farnsworth, a dirt road, and travel 1.4 miles to unmarked trailhead near a wooden bridge. There is limited parking by roadside.

From East Brownfield (junction of Rtes. 160 and 113), travel south 2.2 miles to Farnsworth Road. Turn left and follow earlier directions to unmarked trailhead.

Firewarden's Trail

Pleasant Mountain, Denmark, Maine

Type of trail:	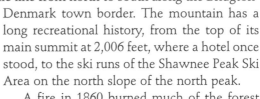
Also used by:	Hikers, backcountry skiers, snowmobilers on portions
Distance:	5.0 miles round-trip
Terrain:	Moderate snowshoe that increases in intensity to a fire tower; outstanding Presidential views
Trail difficulty:	More difficult
Surface quality:	Unpacked
Time:	5 hours
Food and facilities:	No water or rest rooms are available on this trek. Food and sustenance can be found on Bridgton's Main Street with a grocery store and a few restaurants, including the Chinese cuisine of Ruby Food (207–647–8890). There are several hotels in the area, including the aptly named Pleasant Mountain Inn on Route 302 (207–647–4505). Sportshaus (207–647–5100) on Route 302, near the access road to the Shawnee Peak Ski Area, has snowshoe rentals.
Phone numbers:	The Bridgton Chamber of Commerce can be reached at (207) 647–3472.

Surrounded as it is by farms, lakes, ponds, and fields, Pleasant Mountain rises above this beautiful rural expanse like a hulking mass. The mountain runs on a 4.0-mile line from north to south along the Bridgton-Denmark town border. The mountain has a long recreational history, from the top of its main summit at 2,006 feet, where a hotel once stood, to the ski runs of the Shawnee Peak Ski Area on the north slope of the north peak.

A fire in 1860 burned much of the forest on the ledgy mountain, which now affords many outstanding views. From 1873 to 1907, a hotel rested on the main summit, then called House Peak. Now, a fire tower stands there instead. Trails with varying trailheads are scattered all over the mountain. Aside from the main summit, at least six other cones

Snowshoers will find fire towers, like the one atop Pleasant Mountain, on a few Maine peaks.

MOUNTAIN

N

1800

1300

1400

1500

1836

1300

Firewarden's Trail

Lookout Tower
FINISH

1100

1200

800

600

Firewarden's Trail
Scale: 1:15,250 or 4.15" = 1 mile

TRAIL

START

From the top of Pleasant Mountain, the views extend into western Maine and the Presidentials of New Hampshire.

along the ridge have names, according to the Appalachian Mountain Club's *Maine Mountain Guide*.

The Firewarden's Trail, sometimes called the Fire Tower Trail, follows an old carriage road and then a jeep road to the summit, from which there are outstanding views into the shimmering lakes and ponds of western Maine and the rippling Presidential peaks into New Hampshire. A fire tower stands on the summit, but it is boarded during the winter. A few antenna arrays are visible too. Nonetheless, the open summit is a panoramic stage for the skier and snowshoer.

Snowshoers will enjoy the trek, as will backcountry skiers with experience. Cross-country skis aren't a good idea if you go beyond the cabin at the 1.3-mile mark. Backcountry skiers can skin up the mountain and play through the trees on the way down.

Directions at a glance

0.0 Leave via the unmarked trail by a gate. After sign, take left fork and cross brook, following trail along north bank of brook. Expect trail to narrow.

1.3 Reach warden's cabin.

2.3 Blue-blazed Bald Peak Trail is on the left.

2.5 Reach summit and fire tower; return via same trail.

The Firewarden's Trail is sheltered from the wind and doesn't provide much for views until you reach the summit. The trail begins at an unlocked gate. Go in a few hundred yards, you see a sign on the left-hand side, then take the left fork before the trail crosses a brook. The first 1.3 miles is a blend of an easy to moderate climb as the trail crosses a brook and bends to the right, climbing the north bank of the brook. The wide trail, a truck road, narrows dramatically as you reach the warden's cabin at 1.3 miles. The trail then rises rather steadily as it leads to the summit. About 2.3 miles into the trek, the blue-blazed Bald Peak Trail enters from the left. Up ahead, look for a shelter off the trail to the right before the final 0.2-mile climb to the summit and the fire tower.

How to get there

From Fryeburg, travel 7.0 miles east on Route 302 to Warren Road (Fire Lane 37), turn right and follow Warren Road 1.2 miles (stay right at junctions) to a farmhouse. The trail leaves from the left side of the road.

From Bridgton, travel 2.6 miles west on Route 302 from the Shawnee Peak Ski Area access road. Turn left on Warren Road, Fire Lane 37 (just beyond Harvest Hills). Travel 1.2 miles. Trail is on left by farmhouse.

Douglas Mountain

Douglas Mountain Preserve, Sebago, Maine

Type of trail:	🐾
Also used by:	Hikers
Distance:	0.5-mile trail; optional 0.75-mile Nature Trail
Terrain:	A short snowshoe to a stone tower at the top of a tiny peak, offering grand views
Trail difficulty:	Easiest
Surface quality:	Unpacked
Time:	1 hour ·
Food and facilities:	Save for toilets, there are no other facilities at the Douglas Mountain Preserve. There are several hotels in the area, including the aptly named Pleasant Mountain Inn on Route 302 in Bridgton (207–647–4505). Sportshaus (207–647–5100) on Route 302, near the access road to the Shawnee Peak Ski Area, has snowshoe rentals. You can get something to eat at the Subway in Bridgton.
Phone numbers:	You can reach the Bridgton Chamber of Commerce at (207) 647–3472; while the Sebago Town Office is at (207) 787–2457.

Want easy? Think Douglas Mountain. Want views that stretch to the White Mountains, Pleasant Mountain, and the Atlantic Ocean? Think Douglas Mountain on a clear day.

Located west of Sebago Lake, tiny 1,146-foot Douglas Mountain gives snowshoers excellent vistas for minimal effort. The highest of the Saddleback Hills, the Douglas Mountain Preserve sits atop an area that presents views of western Maine and more. In summer the three trails at the preserve are well used by hikers looking for that quick and easy rush. In winter the same can be had, and there appears to be more solitude. For new snowshoers, families, and those who might have slept in on a Sunday morning, this is the route.

In under a half hour, you can be at a stone tower that is a gateway to the horizon.

The Douglas Mountain Preserve is under the auspices of the town of Sebago. The Nature Conservancy purchased the 169 acres in 1971 and held on to the land until 1997. At one time, Douglas Mountain was farmed like much of the land in western Maine. The mountain derived its name from brothers who settled on its slopes in the 1830s. Over the years, the property changed hands. The Douglas Inn once

Douglas Mountain
Scale: 1:10,000 or 6.33" = 1 mile

An inscribed stone at the top of Douglas Mountain is a reminder that all who visit should enjoy. The Latin translates to "Not for one, but for all."

stood at the base of the mountain. In its heyday, the early 1900s, the inn was a top-notch retreat for artists and writers. The hotel was consumed by fire in 1928.

A New York surgeon, Dr. William Blackman, literally changed the face of the mountain in 1925 by helping to construct the 16-foot stone tower that is at the peak's summit. As you snowshoe up the mountain, imagine oxen hauling water, cement, and stones to the top of the mountain to build that tower. That's how it was done.

The tower, which has a chain-link fence on the roof, houses a panoramic display that helps visitors identify the surrounding natural landmarks. From the top, spin around and enjoy one of the most fantastic 360s in the area. Mount Washington is easy to spot 30 miles away. Look for Sebago Lake and even Portland.

Two stone pillars near the parking lot mark the beginning of your walk on the hill. You'll find a registration box there too. Sign in and leave a donation if you are so inclined. The trails pass through a forest of conifers and mixed hardwoods. Familiar trees, like white pine, red spruce, hemlock, red oak, red maple, and white birch, grow on the preserve. Dr. Blackman did more than change the landscape with a tower, he also planted some unusual trees for the area—Douglas fir and white fir. The good doctor's hobby was collecting trees.

Begin the trek through the stone columns and climb steadily through the woods for some 600 feet. The trail levels out. Then you'll come to a fork: The Ledges Trail breaks left and is a slightly shorter path to the summit. However, it has a few steep pitches and bare ledges that can be icy in winter. The Woods Trail drops a tad to the right. Take it and you'll soon be at the summit. Look for a boulder at the summit inscribed with the Latin phrase, NON SIBI SED OMNIBUS. Translated, it means, "not for one, but for all."

After exploring the tower, consider snowshoeing the 0.75-mile Nature Trail, which leads into the woods on the south side of Douglas Mountain. The orange-blazed loop zigs and zags its way along with informational signs about the forest. Its views of the Sebago Lake region are particularly good.

Directions at a glance

0.0 Leave through the stone pillars by the parking area.

0.1 Bear right on the Woods Trail.

0.3 Reach summit and stone tower.

For the optional Nature Trail, go to the right along the orange-blazed 0.75-mile trail from the tower. To return, follow Woods Trail. (Avoid Ledges Trail, which is steep and icy.)

At 0.5 mile from summit, stay straight and travel 0.1 mile back to parking area.

How to get there

From East Baldwin, it is about 5.0 miles to Dyke Mountain Road. First travel on Route 11, then straight on 107. Turn left on Dyke Mountain Road. At 0.9 mile, turn left on Tower Road. The parking area is about 0.5 mile up on the left. The parking area is at the top of a very narrow and winding road. There is limited parking in winter. Be cognizant of the adjacent property owners and heed the NO PARKING signs that are posted along the road. Park in the parking area only.

Sabattus Mountain
Lovell, Maine

Type of trail:	(icon)
Also used by:	Hikers
Distance:	1.6 miles round-trip
Terrain:	Short and easy climb to summit with expansive views from cliff face
Trail difficulty:	Easiest
Surface quality:	Ungroomed
Time:	1½ hours
Food and facilities:	There are no facilities at the trailhead. Sportshaus (207–647–5100), Route 302 in Bridgton, has snowshoe rentals. You can get last-minute snack or a posttrek meal at the Center Lovell Market and Restaurant on Route 5 in Center Lovell. For overnights, try the Center Lovell Inn and Restaurant on Route 5 in Center Lovell (207–925–1575 or 800–777–2698). The owners won the inn in an essay contest!
Phone numbers:	The Bridgton Chamber of Commerce can be reached at (207) 647–3472.

Sabattus Mountain is a little mountain with big views. At less than a mile to the summit, snowshoers have a short, easy climb to expansive views from the ledges of its southwest face. Hills and mountains undulate from the ledges. Alpine slopes fall away in the distance. Lakes and ponds stand frozen in the cold of winter. Take in the views of the countryside from the Baldfaces to Pleasant Mountain.

Sabattus is overseen by the Maine Department of Conservation. Public access to the top of the mountain is regulated by a partnership between the Maine Bureau of Parks and Lands and the Greater Lovell Land Trust. The trail, through a mixed forest with pines and birches, gains some 600 feet in elevation to the top at 1,253 feet.

The trail, not blazed, leaves the parking area and enters the woods. In about 100 yards, the path, marked by

Directions at a glance

0.0 Leave the trailhead. Follow brown trail signs as trail swings right and crosses brook via small bridge.

0.3 The trail swings left.

0.8 Push beyond false summit to reach the final summit, then return via same trail.

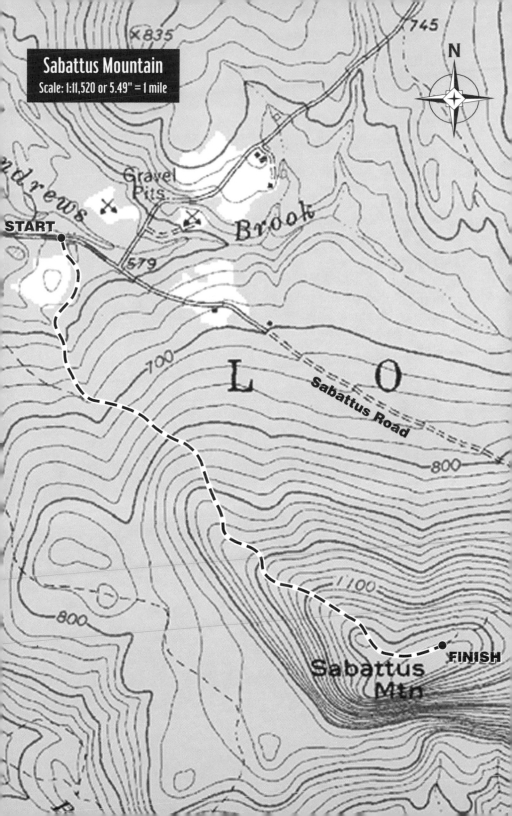

Sabattus Mountain
Scale: 1:11,520 or 5.49" = 1 mile

N

×835

745

Gravel Pits

Brook

START

579

700

L   O

Sabattus Road

800

800

1100

Sabattus Mtn

FINISH

brown trail signs, swings to the right and crosses a brook via a two-plank bridge. The crossing is easy. The wide trail continues at an easy grade for about 0.3 mile before bearing hard to the left. When it does, the grade becomes steeper, but is still a relatively easy one. When pausing, look behind you for mountain views.

The trail reaches a false summit initially, then dips down rather gently before the final push to the top. Near the top is a site where an old fire tower once stood. Now only the base of its legs remains. Though the summit is mostly wooded, the southwest ledges afford wonderful views. Explore the mountain top, searching out the vistas of nearby mountain ranges. Return to the parking area by the same trail.

How to get there

From Lovell, continue north on Route 5 to Center Lovell. At 0.7 mile from the Center Lovell Market and Restaurant, turn right on Sabattus Road. Travel 1.5 miles and take the right fork. In 0.6 mile, turn right into the parking area for Sabattus Mountain.

Goose Eye Trail
Riley, Maine

Type of trail:	⬭
Also used by:	Hikers
Distance:	6.4 miles round-trip
Terrain:	Mountainous terrain that heads above treeline
Trail difficulty:	Most difficult
Surface quality:	Unpacked
Time:	6 hours
Food and facilities:	This is a remote snowshoe trek. No food or water is available so bring plenty. There are no toilets either. Food and last-minute items are plentiful along Route 2 in Gorham, New Hampshire. Because the summit of this trek is above tree line, bring crampons. If you are famished after the trip and can't wait to return to Maine, try the buffet at the Fortune Cookie (603–466–2828) on 310 Main Street in Gorham, New Hampshire, next to the Gorham Motor Inn (603–466–3381). Snowshoes can be rented in Gorham, New Hampshire, from Moriah Sports, 101 Main Street (603–466–5050).
Phone numbers:	For more information, contact the White Mountain National Forest's Evans Notch Ranger District, RR2, P. O. Box 2270, Bethel, Maine 04217. Telephone is (207) 824–2134.

Remote and wild is the land that straddles the Maine-New Hampshire border along the mighty Androscoggin River. This is moose and logging country. Goose Eye Mountain is part of the Mahoosuc Range, which includes Old Speck among its stellar peaks. One of the hundred highest in New England, Goose Eye's cone-shaped summit at 3,870 feet has scenic, panoramic views of two states.

The Maine side of the range appears more isolated than the New Hampshire side, where lumber company roads feed into the remote areas. Access to the Goose Eye Trail is from the New Hampshire side along a dirt road. The trail, maintained by the Appalachian Mountain Club, passes through land owned by a paper company. There are no permits needed to travel through. Just pack out what you pack in.

Though Goose Eye begins in New Hampshire, it then crosses into Maine, where some of the finest views in the range can be had. From the lofty summit, see across to Grafton Notch and Old Speck. The

Goose Eye Trail

Scale: 1:18,190 or 3.48" = 1 mile

slopes of the Sunday River Ski Area are in the distance. From the summit of Goose Eye, have a bird's-eye view of the mountain's east peak just below.

Most of the trail winds through the woods and is sheltered from the wind. But that changes on the summit. Whenever traveling above tree line, take extra caution (and crampons, ice axes, ski poles, etc). Depending on the snowpack, the final 100 yards of this trek to the summit can be difficult. The same holds true on the descent from the summit.

First, begin by leaving the parking area along a flat, wide logging road, which also serves as the starting point for the Carlo Col Trail. After about 100 yards, the Goose Eye Trail turns hard left, scrambles down an embankment, and makes a hard right. The trail is blazed in blue and follows a flat logging road through an evergreen tunnel. You'll have a few opportunities to catch a glimpse of the pyramid-shaped cone of Goose Eye. Cross two brooks as the trail continues at an easy grade. Following the second brook crossing, the trail stays straight by a junction (look at the sign), and

Windswept snow sometimes blows across trails, making snowshoers work a bit more for those views.

shortly thereafter it bears right onto another wide road (at about the 0.8-mile mark). At about 100 yards, Goose Eye heads back into cover on the right side. You'll see a sign.

Keep your eyes peeled for moose. They've been spotted in this area before. At about 1.4 miles, you leave New Hampshire and cross into Maine. Chances are the yellow-blazed stone marker will be covered in snow. Of late, there has also been a sign posted to a tree that welcomes winter walkers to the Mahoosuc Range and reminds them that the trail passes through paper company land.

Once in Maine, the trail toughens up and begins a moderate grade through hardwoods. It slabs along the south side of a ridge. The trail ascends more steeply before leveling out for a spell at about the 2.6-mile mark. Try and spot Goose Eye through the trees. The last 0.5 mile is a combination of moderate and steep pitches, with the final 100 yards or so punctuated with ledges that could be slick. Use caution as the tree line is left behind. Once on top, enjoy the accomplishment; safely return to the parking area along the same trail.

How to get there

From Gilead, Maine, travel west on Route 2 to Gorham, New Hampshire, to Route 16 north in Berlin. At the traffic light, turn right over James Cleveland Bridge. After the bridge, the road becomes Unity Street, bears left, and crosses traffic lights. Stay straight. Unity crosses train tracks and becomes Hutchins Street. At about 2.0 miles from Route 16, turn right on the unmarked Success Pond Road. There is a brown sign that reads OHRV parking 1 mile. Success Pond Road is a dirt road suitable for four-wheel drive. Follow it 8.3 miles. The trailhead for the Goose Eye Trail is on the right. Beware of logging trucks on the remote Success Pond Road.

Directions at a glance

0.0 From parking area, follow sign to Goose Eye Trail. After about 100 yards, turn left on Goose Eye Trail, followed closely by a hard turn right. Follow blue blazes and cross two brooks.

0.8 Bear right on Goose Eye Trail.

1.4 Cross border from New Hampshire into Maine.

3.2 Reach Goose Eye Mountain summit. Return via Goose Eye Trail.

5.0 Cross border from Maine back into New Hampshire.

5.6 Bear left on Goose Eye Trail.

6.3 Turn left on Goose Eye Trail. In 100 yards, turn right to return to parking area.

Little Deer, Big Deer Loop

White Mountain National Forest, Stow, Maine

Type of trail: ⬤

Also used by: Hikers

Distance: 3.3-mile combined loop; optional Little Deer Loop only 1.8 miles

Terrain: Hilly snowshoe trip in a notch less taken during the winter months

Trail difficulty: More difficult

Surface quality: Unpacked

Time: 3½ hours

Food and facilities: The Stow Corner Store (207–697–2943) on Route 113, an eclectic general store, is the closest outpost for snacks and sandwiches. In Fryeburg, try Village Variety on Main Street (207–935–2909). Overnight accommodations are available in Fryeburg at the Admiral Peary House Bed and Breakfast, 9 Elm Street (207–935–3365). There are toilets at the trailhead, but no water. A White Mountain National Forest recreation pass is needed to park at the trailhead. They are available at the Stow Corner Store or from WMNF ranger stations.

Phone numbers: For more information on Evans Notch, contact the White Mountain National Forest's Evans Notch Ranger District, RR 2, P. O. Box 2270, Bethel, Maine 04217. Telephone is (207) 824–2134.

Evans Notch is a mountain pass less traveled in winter. The notch, which straddles the Maine-New Hampshire border, is in the mountains and woods of the White Mountain National Forest. The forest, known for its natural drama and diversity, covers some 775,000 acres. An estimated 4.5 million people visit the forest annually. Most don't travel to the small section (49,346 acres) of the forest in Maine. It is their loss.

One reason that this section is underutilized is that a portion of Route 113 that winds through the notch is closed in winter, severing the pass in half. The unplowed section though can be a playground for all sorts of recreational pursuits, like snowshoeing, cross-country skiing, and mushing. It also is a snowmobile corridor.

Evans Notch has a passive beauty to it. A snowshoe up to Little and Big Deer Hills will reward you with views of the rounded cones of Baldface in New Hampshire—from Little Deer Hill (1,080 feet) and the

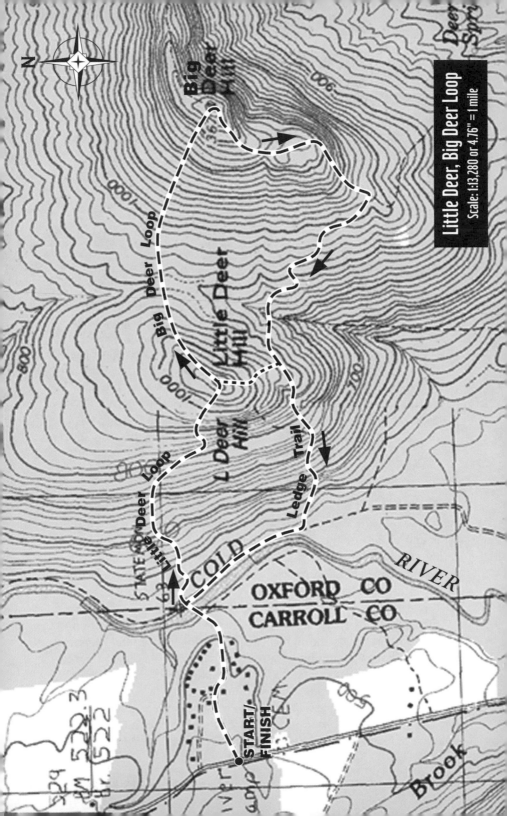

woodlands of the Evergreen Valley in Maine, or from the ledges off the summit of Big Deer Hill (1,367 feet). The views are especially magnificent from the open top of Little Deer Hill. North and South Baldface rise admirably from the low valley floor. Sable and Chandler Mountains hold court to the southwest.

From Big Deer Hill, snowshoe down a ridge that presents extended views into the rippling hills and bodies of water in the distance. Do not be fooled by the gentle appearance of the Deer Hills. You gain nearly 1,000 feet in elevation from the banks of the Cold River to the summit of Big Deer Hill. There are a couple of steep pitches where, depending on the amount of snow, side stepping might be in order.

This trip comprises two loops. You can do both or just the Little Deer Loop (1.8 miles). It all depends on how much time you have.

The trails for these loops are blazed yellow and maintained by the Chatham (N.H.) Trail Association. Though the trek begins in New Hampshire, it quickly enters Maine.

The journey begins at the Baldface parking area, following the sign for Deer Hill via Chester Dam. Wind through the pine forest and snowshoe down to the rock-strewn Cold River, which weaves through the two states. Trek parallel to the chilling water along a gentle, flat part of the trail. Keep your eyes peeled for a fenced-in gazebo on a ridge overlooking the water. Come to the Chester Dam. An engraved boulder tells that the dam is a memorial to Mabel C. Chester, a lover of the Cold River Valley. Maine is just on the other side of the river. Notice the cute tea cups etched in the trail sign. That pathway to the right leads to the Appalachian Mountain Club's Cold River Camp. Don't go that way. Instead, go left and cross the river on the dam. It might be a good idea to take off your snowshoes.

On the other side, turn right and pass a stone marker that indicates the Maine–New Hampshire border. Cross back into the Pine Tree State, navigate a brief knoll, and find yourself at another signed junction (at 0.4 mile). Stay left at the junction and follow the sign that reads LITTLE DEER, BIG DEER, begin a moderate climb. The view opens up along ledges that lead to excellent views from the summit of Little Deer Hill at 0.9 mile. A trail signpost stands atop Little Deer. It is possible to loop back to the trailhead at this junction without visiting Big Deer. Do this by dropping down to the left to a junction via the trail marked as Deer Hill Spring/Forest Service Road. Get to a junction and turn right. Pick up the Big Deer Loop (see Directions at a glance).

If you plan to continue to Big Deer, drop back into the woods and down into a saddle between the two peaks. Reaching the sag, the trail then ascends, steeply at times, to the wooded summit of Big Deer.

Views into New Hampshire can be had through the trees. Continue just beyond the summit to the south ridge, where a few outlooks also afford excellent views.

The trail jabs to the left and descends quickly along a ridge with farms and fields in the distance. At a junction (1.9 miles), a sign points left to Forest Road 9. Turn right instead, following the yellow blazes and continue descending. The trail comes to a T at a wide logging road (2.0 miles). An arrow points to the right. Follow it for about 0.1 mile. Another arrow will point right. Follow it.

The trail descends into another sag and then climbs back up to Little Deer. The path leads to another junction at 2.3 miles. If you turn right, you get back up on Little Deer. But stay straight to return to the parking area. The trail descends somewhat moderately and comes to a stone wall, which the trail follows for a spell. The Ledge Trail enters at a junction, but stay straight for Cold River, crossing a couple of open ledges. The journey flattens at a junction where you take a right, following along the Cold River. At mile 3.0, you'll soon spot a familiar junction. Turn left toward the river and pass the marker back into New Hampshire. The dam and river reappear. Cross the dam again, turn right, following the signs back to the Baldface parking area.

How to get there

From Fryeburg, travel north on the meandering Route 113 for 17.8 miles and turn right into the Baldface trailhead parking area.

Directions at a glance

0.0 Leave parking area, on trail marked "Deer Hills via Chester Dam" and turn left at sign.

0.3 Turn left and cross Chester Dam after crossing dam, turn right.

0.4 Stay left at junction and follow trail with sign to Little Deer Hill.

0.9 Reach summit of Little Deer Hill. Follow sign left to Big Deer Hill.

1.6 Reach summit of Big Deer Hill. Descend via the yellow-blazed trail (jabbing left).

1.9 Sign points left to FR 9 but turn right instead.

2.0 At T, turn right on wide path by arrow.

2.1 Turn right by arrow.

2.3 Stay straight and follow signs to Cold River and parking area.

2.5 At Ledge Trail, stay straight and follow signs to Cold River.

2.7 Turn right at sign saying Little Deer/Big Deer Spring via loop.

3.0 Turn left at junction. Follow back to dam and cross back over.

3.1 Turn right and follow sign to Baldface parking lot 0.3 mile away.

On a map, it appears the trailhead is handily accessed from Gilead in the northern end of the notch. Do not attempt this unless you want to ski or snowshoe several miles to the Baldface trailhead. Portions of Route 113 are closed in winter. Trail access is only attainable from the southern end of pass in winter.

Gilsland Farm Sanctuary's North Meadow Trail
Falmouth, Maine

Type of trail:	▬▬ ●
Also used by:	Walkers
Distance:	1.2-mile loop
Terrain:	Flat to rolling trails winding through the pleasant paths outside of Maine's largest city
Trail difficulty:	Easiest
Surface quality:	Unpacked
Time:	1 hour
Food and facilities:	Plenty of food and posttrek fare is available in nearby Portland. Near the Maine Mall in South Portland, there are lots of choices like Pizzeria Uno (207–780–8667). The Gilsland Farm Sanctuary and Environmental Center is open to the public free of charge open from dawn until dusk. The visitors center, with its Nature Store and exhibits, is open Monday through Saturday from 8:30 A.M. to 5:00 P.M. and on Sunday from noon until 5:00 P.M. Winter workshops are offered throughout the season on a number of subjects, from identifying animal tracks to learning the calls of birds. Call the center for more information (207–781–2330). Snowshoe rentals are available at the center, but cross-country ski rentals are not. Bring your own. Toilets, water and hot tea are available at the center. Portland has a wealth of overnight accommodations. There is a Holiday Inn (207–774–5601) off I–95 (exit 8).
Phone numbers:	Contact the Gilsland Farm Sanctuary and Environmental Center, 118 U.S. Route 1, P.O. Box 6009, Falmouth, Maine 04105 at (207) 781–2330.

In winter, plump little chickadees and bright red cardinals peck leisurely at the feeders. Out in the meadow, secretive ring-necked pheasants hide in the low bush. Annually, the meadow is hayed in the waning

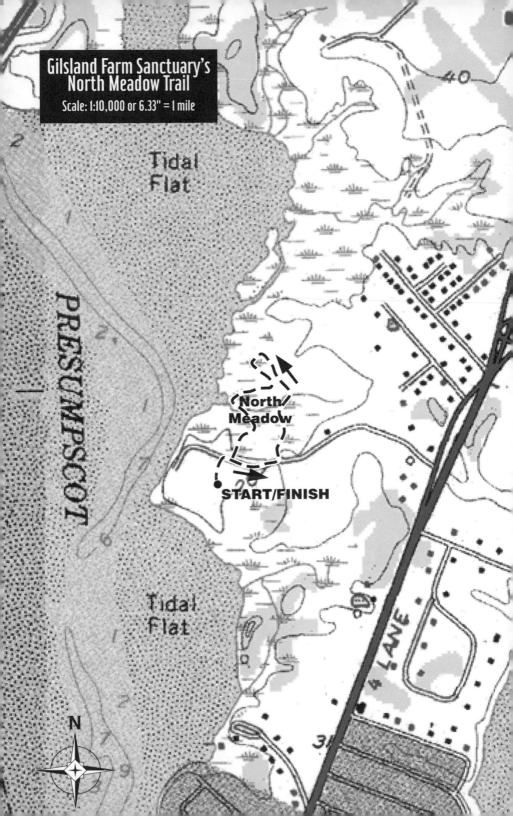

Gilsland Farm Sanctuary's
North Meadow Trail

Scale: 1:10,000 or 6.33" = 1 mile

Tidal
Flat

PRESUMPSCOT

North
Meadow

START/FINISH

Tidal
Flat

LANE

N

40

2

2

1

2

2

1

2

7

6

2

2

1

9

1

7

9

3

Snowshoe hares are sometimes spotted along the trails of the Gilsland Farm Sanctuary in Falmouth. Also keep an eye out for the snowshoe deer, a creation of playful snowshoers.

days of summer. In winter, flocks of Canada geese forage under the snow for fuel to continue their flights. The woods, meadows, and salt marshes are home to the snowshoe hares whose tracks can be spotted all over the sixty-five-acre wildlife sanctuary. Eagle-eyed visitors might even see the white hares resting in their elusive hiding spots. Animals need to eat, and the red fox is no exception. By chance, they might be seen stalking their winter rations—voles, rabbits, and mice.

Owned and managed by the Maine Audubon Society, the Gilsland Farm Sanctuary and Environmental Center is an enjoyable winter playground for all levels of outdoor pursuits. The 2.5 miles of gentle trails are easy to follow. Conveniently placed benches welcome rest, reflection, and picnic lunches. Just minutes from downtown Portland, the sanctuary is a place where the snow meets the sea. Snowshoe or ski through a grove of hemlocks and oaks while listening to the commerce of the sea. Lose yourself among the stands of white ash, birch, and maples. Then gaze from a bluff over the Presumpscot Estuary at the Portland skyline. The sanctuary is a place to get comfortable with your winter feet and maybe even learn a thing or two about the world outdoors. Kids, families, and those out looking for a simple outing will enjoy it here.

Thousands of years before modern-day skiers and snowshoers romped on the trails through the woods, the Wabanaki Indians and their ancestors hunted and fished the area by the estuary's tidal flats. The estuary is where the waters of the Sebago Lake drainage meet Casco Bay. Early residents enjoyed bountiful shellfish, waterfowl, and mammals. English settlers arrived in the 1630s and divided up the land, turning it into farms. Some 300 years later, a Portland lawyer named David Moulton bought the property as a summer hideaway. A dedicated conservationist, he left the farm and surroundings to his daughter on his death. She then donated the property to the Maine Audubon Society.

Three loop trails, with a few connectors and spurs, are showcased on the property. All three are handily marked and leave from outside the visitors center (consult its colorful trail map). The largest loop, the North Meadow Trail, measures 1.2 miles and winds threw a grove of oaks and hemlocks before opening up into a meadow. Look for the barn before circling around by residential homes. The loop edges by the estuary and affords views out onto it.

Directions at a glance

0.0 Leave by the main trailhead via the North Meadow Trail.

0.1 Turn right on North Meadow Trail.

0.3 Cross bridge and bear right at fork toward barn.

0.4 Turn left through meadow.

0.9 Turn right and cross bridge.

1.1 Turn left toward parking area.

About half the distance of North Meadow is the Pond Meadow Trail (0.6 mile). The trail slips through maples and ash before leading down to a pond.

The West Meadow Loop (0.7 mile) encircles a meadow over a bluff that looks down to the water and over to Portland. Two spur trails lead to a couple of blinds that allow you to observe the winter waterfowl.

How to get there

From Portland, take I–295 north to exit 9. Travel on U.S. Route 1 1.7 miles and turn right on Gilsland Farm Road. Follow the road to the sanctuary's parking area.

From the north, take I–95/295 to exit 10. Turn left on Bucknam Road. At the stoplight, turn right onto U.S. Route 1 and travel south for about 1.0 mile. Pass the blinking light at the intersection of Routes 1 and 88 and turn right on Gilsland Farm Road.

Salt Hay Loop at Laudholm Farm

Wells National Estuarine Research Reserve, Wells, Maine

Type of trail:	▬▬ ⬭
Also used by:	Walkers
Distance:	2.4-mile loop
Terrain:	Mostly flat with a few short ascents on the rolling hills near the coast
Trail difficulty:	Easiest
Surface quality:	Untracked, but skiers make their own tracks
Time:	2 hours
Food and facilities:	The visitor center at Laudholm Farm is found in a nineteenth-century farmhouse. A gift shop and exhibits are housed there. Rest rooms and water are available. The visitor center is open from 10:00 A.M. to 4:00 P.M. Monday through Saturday, and on Sunday from noon until 4:00 P.M. The trails are open every day from 8:00 A.M. until 5:00 P.M. There is no parking fee during winter. Cross-country ski and snowshoe rentals can be had from the Kittery Trading Post (800–587–6246), Route 1, Kittery. After visiting the farm, fill up again at the very close Maine Diner on Route 1 (207–646–4441). Many of the hotels in Wells take a winter siesta. One that doesn't is the Seabreeze Motel (207–646–4301) on Route 1.
Phone numbers:	The phone number for the Laudholm Farm is (207) 646–4521. The phone number for the Wells National Estuarine Research Reserve is (207) 646–1555.

Maine's deep woods are thought of as wild and remote. But there are those who relish exploring the state's miles of rocky and jagged coastline that parallel the untamed sea. There are places where the snow meets the sea. One such spot is the 7.0 miles of trails at Laudholm Farm at the Wells National Estuarine Research Reserve. Shoreland, marshes, uplands, and estuarine waters are all part of the 1,600-acre reserve, which is home to wide variety of wildlife, from shorebirds to white-tailed deer. If ever there was a trail network that guarantees your seeing wildlife, this is it. Even in winter, shorebirds frequent the two estuaries by the saltwater farm. The salt waters of the ocean mingle with the freshwater of the land. White-tail deer do frequent the area, though they may be too quick for those wanting to capture the moment on film. Fox can be seen. The snow acts as a canvas on which deer leave their imprints. Fresh scat is frequently seen on

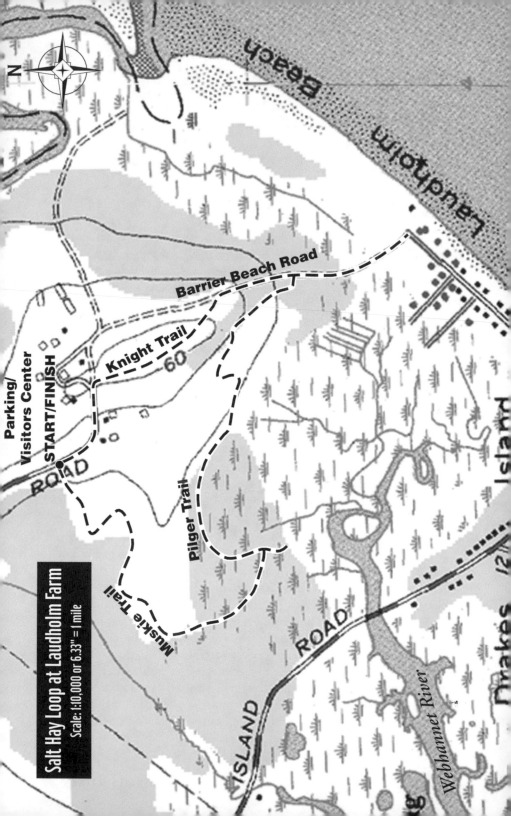

N

Laudholm Beach

Barrier Beach Road

Knight Trail 60

Parking/
Visitors Center

START/FINISH

ROAD

Pilger Trail

Muskie Trail

Island

ISLAND ROAD

Webhannet River

Drakes

Salt Hay Loop at Laudholm Farm
Scale: 1:10,000 or 6.33" = 1 mile

the trails that wind through the northernmost part of the reserve.

Two rivers—the Little and Webhannet Rivers—meet the Atlantic Ocean on the reserve, which was established in 1986 as part of the National Estuarine Reserve System. The purpose of the reserve is to serve as a natural outdoor laboratory for the study of the estuarine environment. In the nonsnow months, various work-shops and programs are open to the public. Things slow down a bit in winter. The visitor center does house exhibits. Visitors can learn about the farm, first settled in 1643, home to only four families in its 350-year history.

Seven miles of trails await snowshoers and skiers at Laudholm Farm in Wells. The system is a part of a research facility that studies estuaries.

Many first-time visitors to the reserve head straight to the sea via the Knight Trail and Barrier Beach Road. Out and back, this is an easy 1.4-mile jaunt from the visitor center to the crashing waves of the Atlantic. You pass snow-covered fields with shrubs popping out as well as an apple orchard. Snowshoe or ski through a marshy area that leads to rocky shores near private homes. Respect the privacy by staying on the right-of-way.

Ever snowshoe or ski on a board-walk? The Salt Marsh Loop, a 1.3-mile circuit, takes visitors on the Laird-Norton Trail and the wooden pathway that runs along the edge of freshwater uplands. The easy outing consists of the Knight, Laird-Norton, and Old Cart Path Trails.

Two scenic overlooks are part of the gentle Salt Hay Loop. In winter, families come to snowshoe and ski it. The trail begins just outside the

Directions at a glance

0.0 Leave the Laudholm Farm Visitor Center on the Muskie Trail, heading southwest.

1.0 Turn left on Pilger Trail. Spur trail on right leads to Drakes Island Overlook.

1.6 Turn left on Barrier Beach Road/Knight Trail. A right leads to the beach, 0.2 mile.

1.7 Bear left on the Knight Trail and follow it back to the visitor center.

visitor center and cuts downward along the Muskie Trail through the fields and into the woods. From time to time, a well-placed bench invites rest. The Muskie Trail winds through the woods and follows the area along trees and field. Where the Muskie and Pilger Trails meet, a short spur trail leads to the Drakes Island Overlook, which provides you with views of the brackish marsh by the Webhannet River. A nearby sign provides a bit of a science lesson about the migratory paths taken by birds. Continue left on the Pilger Trail as it winds a bit along the edge of lowlands and fields. Look for posted sign with cartoon-like images of deer and fox. It was near one of these signs that the cartoons came to life as two white-tail deer. The Pilger Trail snakes downward as it nears the intersection with the Barrier Beach Road. Turn left and follow the wide Beach Road back to the visitor center. It will lead to the Knight Trail, which also has some convenient benches at the top of a hill for viewing the Webhannet Overlook. The trail then leads to the starting point by the yellow visitor center.

How to get there

From the Maine Turnpike, take exit 2 to Wells. Turn left on Routes 9 and 109 (south). Turn left on Route 1 and drive 1.5 miles. Turn right at second blinking light onto Laudholm Farm Road. Go 0.4 mile and bear left at fork, following signs to the area. Turn right into the reserve.

Sebago Lake State Park's Songo River Trail

Sebago Lake State Park, Naples, Maine

Type of trail:	▬▬▬▬ ⬤
Also used by:	Walkers
Distance:	4.0 miles round-trip
Terrain:	Flat
Trail difficulty:	Easiest
Surface quality:	Unpacked, but groomed by snowmobilers after storms
Time:	2 hours
Food and facilities:	Rest rooms are located along the route. Picnic tables are available too. Bring your own water. The Raymond Shopping Center on Route 302 is a good spot to pick up last minute items, and there are a few convenience stores along the way to the park on Route 302. The White Pines Motel (207–655–3345) is conveniently located in Raymond, while Deb's Sebago Diner (207–655–2900) on Route 302 has down-home cooking for the posttrek meal.
Phone numbers:	The phone number for Sebago Lake State Park is (207) 693–6231.

Sebago Lake is a study in contrasts. During summer, the 1,300-acre state park, which rests on the lake's northern shores, is aflutter with activity. Lifeguards watch swimmers in the clear waters. Hamburgers and hot dogs sizzle on the grill. Rangers give interpretive talks. The 300 campsites can be filled.

In winter, 5.0 miles of trails greet the cross-country skier and snowshoer. Solitude can be found midweek along the evergreens. But on weekends, the park is popular (though not even close to its summer use), with a ranger saying that the parking areas at the trailheads can be as much as two-thirds full.

Sebago Lake is the state's second largest lake. Located some 20 miles northwest of Portland, it also provides that city's water supply. Freshwater fish like togue and salmon live in the lake. The lake is ringed by the neighboring hills and inundated with vacation homes of all shapes, forms, and pedigrees.

Winter is quiet in Sebago Lake State Park. Blazes of blue diamonds mark the trails, which basically fall on either side of the park access road. At one time, the road into the park wasn't plowed and became part of the trail system. But the private landowners who abut the park wanted year-round access to the road, so rangers cut new trails for skiers and snowshoers.

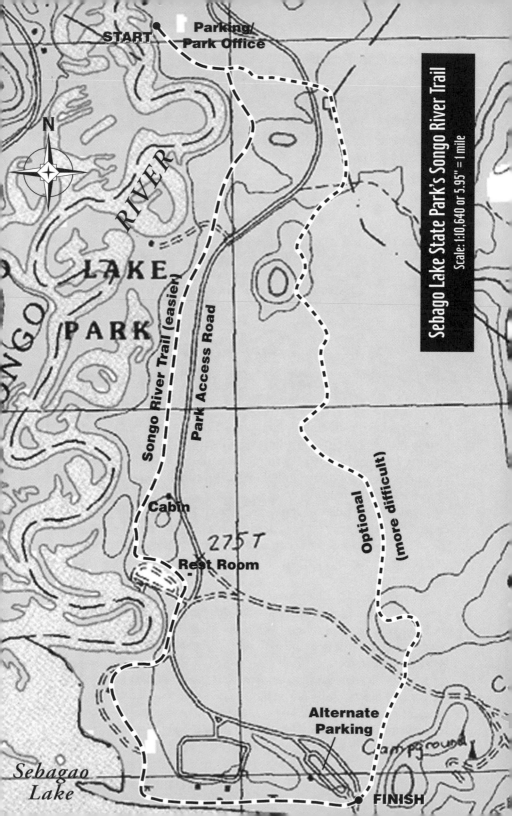

START

Parking/
Park Office

N

RIVER

LAKE

PARK

ONGO

Songo River Trail (easier)

Park Access Road

Cabin

275T

Rest Room

Optional

(more difficult)

Sebagao
Lake

Alternate
Parking

FINISH

Sebago Lake State Park's Songo River Trail

Scale: 1:10,640 or 5.95" = 1 mile

The Songo River bends sharply in Sebago Lake State Park. Snowshoers can traipse along water's edge en route to the shores of Sebago Lake.

The trails are not tracked. But skiers use them enough to create their own. After sizeable snowfalls, park employees groom the trails, using a snowmobile. Snowshoers can use the trails, too, but are asked to stay off the ski tracks.

Directions at a glance

0.0 Leave by the trailhead by the northern entrance to the park.

0.3 Turn right at junction.

1.0 Reach cabins and toilet.

2.0 Reach southern parking area and shores of Sebago Lake, return via same route.

The trails on the eastern side of the park access road are a tad more hilly as compared with those on the western side. More snow is needed to play on them as they wind up, down, and over three hills.

Clearly, though, the most scenic and easiest trail is the 2.0-mile stretch that plays a game of cat and mouse with the oxbows of the Songo River. The trail along the river is flat. When it doesn't afford views of the sultry curves in the river, it is wide enough for two to snowshoe or ski abreast through the tall pines. After the 0.25-mile mark, the trail follows a road along the river. There are a couple of vantage points from which to see the river. Near the 1.0-mile mark, cabins shut for the winter are dormant. The trail will then hug the road and river before leading to the lake.

Near the southern end of the trail, paths lead to the lakeshore. The picnic areas are undisturbed. Snow covers the picnic tables and swings. Sebago Lake doesn't freeze completely, so don't venture out onto the ice, especially by the mouth of the Songo River, where currents preclude safe crossing. Admire the beauty from the shores.

The trails at Sebago Lake are blazed in blue. At key intersections, you'll see maps with the familiar "You are here." By keeping the river to one side and the park road to the other, it is fairly easy to navigate the trail along the Songo River.

It is possible to start at either end. The trail seemed easier to find at the northern entrance to the park. The park offices are there.

How to get there

From the junction of Routes 302, 35, and 121 in Raymond, travel 5.5 miles west on Route 302. Turn left on State Park Road. Travel 1.6 miles, then turn left again on the park access road in Sebago Lake State Park. Drive 0.1 mile, and bear right to the first parking area by a trailhead. An alternative trailhead parking area near the lake's shore is about 2.0 miles down the park access road.

Bradbury Mountain State Park's Tote Road Loop

Bradbury Mountain State Park, Pownal, Maine

Type of trail:	▬▬ ▦
Also used by:	Hikers
Distance:	2.6-mile loop; optional Summit Trail, snowshoe only, 0.6-mile round-trip
Terrain:	Hilly and rolling, but the views atop Bradbury Mountain and the ski down make it worth the time.
Trail difficulty:	More difficult
Surface quality:	Groomed after storms. Skiers make their own tracks.
Time:	1½ hours
Food and facilities:	Bradbury Mountain State Park has parking, a playground, pit toilets, and picnic tables. Year-round camping is available. Call the park ranger for reservations. No water available. Trail conditions are posted by the map at the entrance. There is a small fee to use the park. There is a convenience store less than a mile from the park at the junction of Route 9 and Elmwood Road. Next to that is Morgan's Restaurant (207–688–3300). Snowshoe and cross-country ski rentals can be had from L. L. Bean in Freeport (800–341–4341). Freeport also has accommodations.
Phone numbers:	The number for Bradbury Mountain State Park is (207) 688–4712.

In the 1940s, Bradbury Mountain was home to downhill skiing and a rope tow. Now, the nearly 500-acre park has 8.0 miles of cross-country ski and snowshoe trails. If you want to get up to the top of the 484-foot mountain, you've got to do it by your own power.

Bradbury Mountain is the attraction of this state park, one of the five original state parks in Maine. The state bought the parks from the federal government in 1939. The park, located midway between Lewiston-Auburn and Portland, has well-marked trails, complete with blazes and mileage signs.

Though the peak is tiny, the summit views from the top of Bradbury's ledgy summit reach all the way to Casco Bay. The vistas are east to the ocean, out over the wooded countryside, where life seems to slow down a bit. Snowshoers have the quickest route to the summit via the appropriately named Summit Trail. The path climbs 0.3 mile from the parking area trailhead past the ranger station to the top rather quickly.

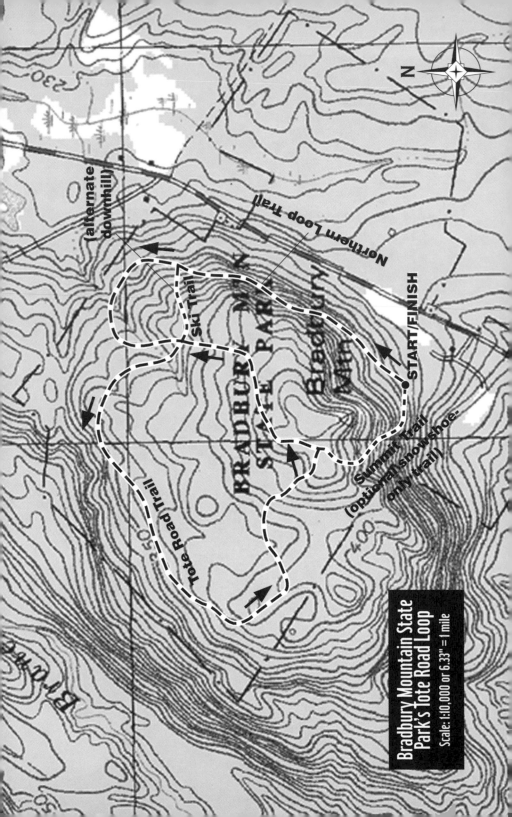

N

(alternate downhill)

Northern Loop Trail

Ski Trail

START/FINISH

BRADBURY MTN. STATE PARK

Bradbury Mtn

Summit Trail (optional snowshoe-only trail)

Tote Road Trail

230

250

400

Bradbury Mountain State Park's Tote Road Loop

Scale: 1:10,000 or 6.33" = 1 mile

The network of winter trails is separated by Route 9. On the eastern side are about 2.0 miles of flat, forested trails. The white-blazed Knight Woods Loop, a 1.0-mile-long circuit, is very easy. When snow is on the light side, that is the trail to do. It is accessible via the Link Trail.

The remaining trails are around the base of the mountain, which was sculpted by a glacier. Skiers can schuss to the top via the Northern Loop, Tote Road, and Boundary Trails.

The Northern Loop Trail begins at the far end of the parking area by the two toilets. The blue-blazed trail is signed and starts as a flat, wooded path, passing by a feld-spar quarry on the left and the softball and vol-leyball area on the right. The quarry was in oper-ation from 1925 to 1929 and produced tons of the mineral for china and pottery. At about 800 feet along, look for the cattle pound on the right. At one time, it was used as a place to house stray sheep, cat-tle, and pigs.

The trail rolls on and parallels a stone wall, a reminder of those set-

The trails at Bradbury Mountain State Park are well-signed with arrows and distances from the parking area to the summit.

tlers who let their pigs get away. At 0.4 mile, the Terrace Trail, which also leads to the summit, enters from the hard left, and the Ski Trail, which connects to both Tote Road and the Northern Loop, is at the left. The Ski Trail is a most difficult 0.2-mile pitch and is a fine alternative heading down the mountain. Stay on the Northern Loop Trail as it swings right and downhill. One-tenth mile later, the orange-blazed Boundary Trail enters right. That trail is a 1.5-mile ski to the summit that skirts the lim-its of the park. At one time it had a steep section that made it most dif-ficult. A bypass is being constructed to make the trail more user friendly and is slated to be ready for the 1999–2000 winter season.

The Northern Loop Trail ascends moderately (use that herringbone) and flattens a bit before coming to a junction with the 1.0-mile-long Tote Road Trail. The Northern Loop continues 0.4 mile to the summit, but instead take a right onto the white-blazed Tote Road Trail and follow it along a stream. The Tote Road rolls and winds its way to the summit, a tunnel of evergreens along the path. The trail increases its grade as it approaches the top of the mountain.

Take a right at the sign and follow it briefly to the open, ledgy summit. The ledge drops quickly, so pay attention. Look for Freeport, Wolfe's Neck, and Portland off in the distance. A map of the trail system is posted at the summit.

Return to the trailhead via the blue-blazed Northern Loop Trail. It descends through the pine. In about 0.3 mile, there is a short spur trail to the right that leads to a bluff with more views of the countryside.

At the junction of the Northern Loop, Tote Road, and Ski Trails, stay on the Northern Loop and follow it back to the trail start. A more difficult alternative is the steep pitch of the Ski Trail. The trail curves to the right at its end where it hooks up again with the Northern Loop Trail. Make that right or make your own sitzmark. The Northern Loop Trail continues back to familiar territory, passing the pound and quarry once again.

How to get there

From I–95, take exit 20 and turn left on Route 136. At the stop sign, turn left on Durham Road and travel 4.6 miles to Pownal. Durham Road undergoes name changes, becoming Pownal Road and then Elmwood Road. At the light at the junction of Elmwood and Route 9, turn right on Route 9 and travel 0.5 miles to Bradbury Mountain State Park to the left.

Directions at a glance

0.0 Leave parking area via the Northern Loop Trail, pass the quarry and rec area, heading northeast. Follow blue blazes.

0.4 Pass the Terrace and Ski Trails and continue straight on the Northern Loop Trail.

0.5 Pass the Boundary Trail and continue straight on the Northern Loop Trail.

0.6 Turn right on the Tote Road Trail. Follow white blazes.

1.6 Turn right for the summit or left on the Northern Loop Trail to return to the parking area.

2.0 Continue straight on Northern Loop Trail at junction.

2.2 Continue straight at junction on Northern Loop Trail to return to parking area.

Harris Farm's Joe Buzzell Lane Loop

Harris Farm Cross-Country Ski Center, Dayton, Maine

Type of trail: ▬▬ ◄ ▣

Distance: 5.0-mile loop; optional Bobcat Loop 3.0 miles, Cold Water Brook Loop 2.0 miles, Maternity Loop 1.0 mile

Terrain: Flat with a few rolling hills through farm and fields

Trail difficulty: All abilities, depending on trail choice; Joe Buzzell Lane Loop and Maternity Loop, easiest; Bobcat Loop and Cold Water Brook Loop, more difficult

Surface quality: Groomed and tracked

Time: 2 hours

Food and facilities: The trail is part of the Harris Farm Cross-Country Ski Center, open Monday through Friday from 9:00 A.M. to dusk, and weekends and holidays from 8:00 A.M. to dusk. Lessons, ski and snowshoe rentals, and pulk rentals are all available at the center. Rest rooms and water are available at the lodge. There is also a snack bar on the second floor of the lodge by the woodstove. It serves up hot chili and the like on weekends. The center also has a retail shop. There is an ice-skating rink and skate rentals. Picnic tables are placed at several intersections along the trails. Sledding is offered on a hill by the lodge. The center is unique in that it is also a working farm, and you can pick up beef, veal, and bottled milk too. In nearby Lyman, the Goodwins Mills General Store (207–499–9999) has last-minute items and that post-ski sandwich.

Phone numbers: The Harris Farm Cross-Country Ski Center can be reached by calling (207) 499–2678.

Snow is the winter crop of several farms in southern Maine. Just ask Bill Harris, who, along with his wife Dixie and their children, run the Harris Farm Cross-Country Ski Center in Dayton. A working dairy farm where skiers sunning themselves on the deck of the second-floor lodge are likely to hear the moos of the one hundred or so cows in the barn, the farm produces dairy products and small vegetables. As Harris likes to say, he has two products, sweet corn and skiing. The boys, as he calls them, tend to the dairy and small vegetables. The farm has been in the family since 1944. In 1988, skiing was added as the winter crop. Instead of harvesting corn, the Harris's tend to skiers and snowshoers on the 26 miles of trails. Generally, the trails are 8 to 12 feet wide. Snowshoers are

Harris Farm's Joe
Buzzell Lane Loop

Scale: 1:11,490 or 5.52" = 1 mile

START/FINISH

Buzzell Road

Bridge

Bridge

N

35

allowed on the entire network and are asked not to step on the tracked sections. Skate skiers account for roughly one-third of the visitors to the network, which comprises 500 acres of the farm and another 500 acres of abutting other landowners' property. About 85 miles from Boston's North Shore, the center attracts day-trippers from the Bay State, as well as Mainers from Scarborough, Kittery, and Portland.

Woods, farm, and fields dominate the landscape. Keep on eye out for deer and wild turkeys. Some 90 percent of skiers at Harris head for the Joe Buzzell Loop (Buzzell was a family that once farmed in these parts) because of its relative ease. But that is not the only trail worth exploring. More advanced skiers like the 3.0-mile Bobcat Loop on the eastern side of the center for its varied rolling terrain. The 2.0-mile more difficult Cold Water Brook Loop is favored by those who ski with their canines. It is affectionately called the "Poop du Loop" because dogs are allowed on that section of trail and the snow isn't too soft. The Maternity Loop is a gentle 1.0-mile loop warm-up that starts outside the barn. It is so named because it is in the pasture where cows give birth to their calves.

The Joe Buzzell Loop is the pathway through the sheltered pine and oak forests. It begins on the west side of the center (across the road). The trip has one big benefit: You can leave your skis on. Sometimes skiers don't like taking those skis off once they've started. Put them on at the trailhead and keep them on.

Wide-open fields are the first elements of the ski, before ducking into the quiet of the woods where a nice gentle dip is waiting. The trail flattens out and is quite easy. Signs are placed at the key intersections. Maps with the familiar "you-are-here" are there too. A note about reading these maps. Know where north is. Know that the sun rises in the east and sets in the west. Not every

Some Maine farms treat snow as a winter crop and open up the woods and fields to cross-country skiers. The Harris Farm Cross-Country Ski Center in Dayton is one example.

trail system has a map with north at the top of the key. Such is the case at Harris.

A couple of tree islands on the trail are good fun. Skiers are given a choice which leg to take; both options end at the same point on the other side.

When not in the woods, the Joe Buzzell trail briefly follows one of the natural springs that helps irrigate the farm and leads to the open, rolling pastures, a nice downhill before wrapping up the ski tour. Top it off with the strawberry-flavored milk. It doesn't get any fresher.

How to get there

From Maine Turnpike, exit 3, head north on Route 35 for 11.5 miles through Goodwins Mills. Bear right onto Gould Road, which intersects with Buzzell Road. Turn right onto Buzzell Road for 1.0 mile to the center.

From Maine Turnpike, exit 4, turn right off exit to Route 111. Travel west to intersection with Route 35. Turn right (north) on Route 35 and travel 4.5 miles through Goodwins Mills (Lyman). Bear right onto Gould Road, which intersects with Buzzell Road. Turn right on Buzzell Road and drive 1.0 mile to the center.

Directions at a glance

0.0 Leave the trailhead on Joe Buzzell Lane (Trail 14), just off Buzzell Road; head southwest.

1.0 Turn left on Joe Buzzell Lane.

1.2 Bear right on Joe Buzzell Lane.

3.2 Turn left on Joe Buzzell Lane.

3.7 Stay straight on Joe Buzzell Lane.

4.9 Turn right on Joe Buzzell Lane and head to lodge.

Wolf Neck Woods State Park

Freeport, Maine

Type of trail:	⬤, ▬▬▬ (portions)
Also used by:	Hikers
Distance:	2.6-mile loop
Terrain:	Wooded trail that overlooks the coast in spots, offering wondrous water vistas
Trail difficulty:	Easiest
Surface quality:	Unpacked
Time:	3 hours
Food and facilities:	Picnic tables and grills are offered at Wolf Neck Woods State Park in winter. Bring your own water. No rest rooms. Parking is limited. Park is close to Freeport; food and facilities are to be found there. The Bow Street Market on Bow Street is a place to stop for food. Afterward, quaff a pint at Gritty McDuff's, Route 1 (207–865–4321). Cross-country ski and snowshoe rentals are available from L. L. Bean, Main Street, Freeport (800–341–4341). Freeport has a number of accommodations, including a Super 8 Motel on Route 1 (207–865–1408).
Phone numbers:	Call the Maine State Information Center (exit 17 off I-95) at (207)846–0833. The number for the Maine Department of Conservation's Bureau of Parks and Lands is (207) 287–3821. Wolf Neck Woods State Park is at (207) 624–6080.

From a waterproof hunting shoe, an empire was born. Freeport is synonymous with Leon Leonwood Bean, better known as L. L. Bean. The giant retailer has its headquarters in Freeport, and a huge retail store, complete with an indoor trout pond, is open twenty four hours a day. Now Freeport has more than one hundred stores in town. It may have lost some of its coastal village charm, but a slice of beauty can be found less than 5.0 miles from the hub of Freeport.

Wolf Neck Woods State Park is more than 200 acres of woods and shoreland near the tip of one of Maine's many midcoast peninsulas. Five miles of trails wind through the forested park and along the rocky shores of Casco Bay and the Harraseeket River. The trails are mostly snowshoe-friendly, but cross-country skiers can find a few to ski on, like the short Old Woods Trail and the unplowed park access road. However, the Casco Bay and Harraseeket Trails, which when linked together make a picturesque jaunt from sea to pines, aren't ideal for skiing.

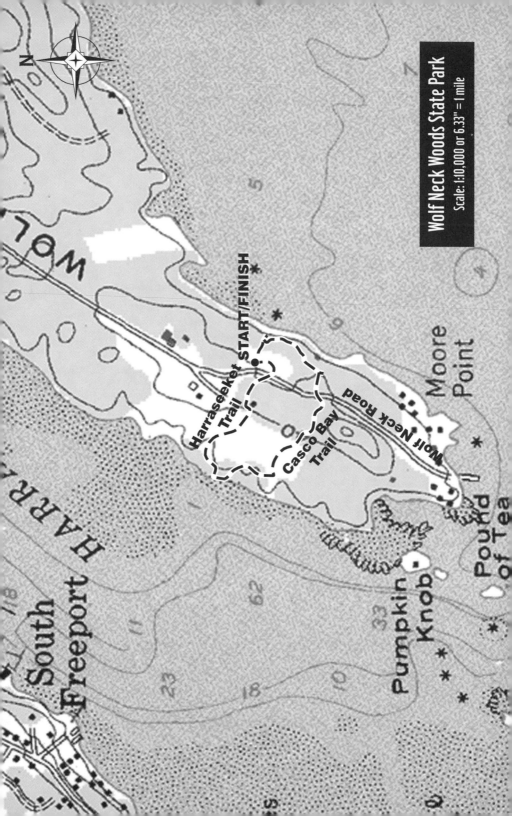

Wolf Neck Woods State Park
Scale: 1:10,000 or 6.33" = 1 mile

N

Harraseeket START/FINISH
Trail

Casco Bay
Trail

Wolf Neck Road

Moore
Point

Pound
of Tea

Pumpkin
Knob

South
Freeport

HARR

WOL

The gate at the park entrance is down during winter, making for limited parking. But enter the park on its wide, forested access road and proceed past the dormant tollbooth and a signboard. The big map board at the trailhead (0.3 mile) details the loops within the park and is the starting point for a 2.0-mile snowshoe that goes for a spell along a most magnificent piece of Maine. Though there are several signs throughout the park naming the various trails and occasional arrows pointing the way, the trails are not blazed. There are also interpretive signs at scenic overlooks and benches on which to rest. There are stairs to negotiate on the Casco Bay Trail (take off the snowshoes) and several easily traveled wooden bridges. Because the park is a popular destination, the trails are usually tracked by previous visitors.

Walk to the left of the signboard, following the sign that points to the shore and Casco Bay Trail. Enter the snow–covered woods, going south. Pass by the pines and the picnic tables that are waiting for the sun of summer. After about 0.1 mile the trail will come to a T with stairs to the left that lead down to the rocky shores. An interpretive sign details the geology of the area. Use the bench and soak up the scene.

The Casco Bay Trail continues to the right at that junction and soon crosses another footbridge. The gently climbing trail has views of Casco Bay. The trail follows the shoreline for about 1,800 feet and offers unsurpassed ocean vistas. In another 0.1 mile, you reach another scenic overlook with sign, stairs, and the sea. This sign notes that the sea and shore are home to a variety of birds, fish, and animals, like mackerel and harbor seals.

The Casco Bay Trail in Wolf Neck Woods State Park follows the rocky coast for about 1,800 feet.

After the second overlook, the trail winds away from the edge of the ocean back into the woods for a spell. The ocean shimmers through the trees, and the path eventually makes it back to one more overlook by a sign pointing to the Small Bog, Hemlock Ridge, and Harraseeket Trails. To the left is a bench, stairs, and an intrepretive sign that points out the islands in the bay. Keep a look out for ice floes with seagulls perched on them. Then continue on to the right of the sign.

The trail then begins to ascend the ridge. The ocean is now behind you. Spruce, pine, and hemlock line the forest. The Small Bog Trail will enter from the right—you stay straight to follow the sign that marks the Hemlock Ridge and Harraseeket Trails. The trail wiggles up and down, passes the Old Woods Trail, which is a 0.3 stretch back to the map board, and heads underneath utility lines. The path goes through an old stone wall before reaching a junction with the Hemlock Ridge and Small Bog Trails. Continue straight and down the hill on the 1.2-mile-long Harraseeket Trail, which has the occasional arrow. The trail crosses Wolf Neck Road and continues directly across the other side. The inland trek reaches water again as the trail parallels the Harraseeket River Estuary. There are a few points to look at on the water and rocky shores. It is a steep drop down to the water so stay away from the edge. For a short stretch the trail is like a rollercoaster. It then takes a sharp right and heads back uphill toward the road again. Cross Wolf Neck Road; the trail continues directly across in the woods. It is now about 0.3 mile back to the map board, then another 0.3 mile back to the closed gate.

Directions at a glance

0.0 Leave from park gate on park access road.

0.3 Reach map signboard and bear left at sign pointing to shore and Casco Bay Trail.

0.4 Come to a T. Turn right to continue on Casco Bay Trail. To the left are stairs leading down to a scenic overlook.

0.5 Turn right at sign for Small Bog, Hemlock Ridge, and Harraseeket Trails.

0.8 Continue straight at the sign marking the Hemlock Ridge and Harraseeket Trails.

1.1 Continue straight on the Harraseeket Trail, paralleling the estuary.

2.0 Turn left and follow the access road back to the closed gate.

How to get there

From I–95, take either exit 19 or 20 to Freeport. Route 1 also goes to Freeport. Route 1 is Main Street in Freeport. Take Bow Street (by L. L. Bean) and travel 2.3 miles. Turn right on Wolf Neck Road and drive 2.1 miles to the parking area on the left. There is limited parking in winter.

Ridge Trail

Maine Audubon Society Mast Landing Sanctuary, Freeport, Maine

Type of trail:	⬬⬬
Also used by:	Hikers
Distance:	1.6-mile loop
Terrain	An easy family outing through the pines and fields of coastal Maine, stopping at an old mill
Trail difficulty:	Easiest
Surface quality:	Ungroomed
Time:	2 hours
Food and facilities:	Picnic tables are located in the parking area. Food and facilities can be found in Freeport. The Bow Street Market on Bow Street is a place to stop for food. Afterward, try Gritty McDuff's, Route 1 (207–865–4321) for a beverage. Cross-country ski and snowshoe rentals are available from L. L. Bean, Main Street, Freeport (800–341–4341). Freeport has a number of accommodations, including a Super 8 Motel (207–865–1408) on Route 1.
Phone numbers:	The Maine Audubon Society Mast Landing Sanctuary is at (207) 781–2330. Call the Freeport Chamber of Commerce at (207) 865–1212 or (800) 865–1994.

The Maine Audubon Society's Mast Landing Sanctuary has about 3.0 miles of trails through forest and fields, just 2.0 miles from downtown Freeport. The trails, which are largely in the cover of the woods, are easy to follow and are good spots for beginning snowshoers or those seeking to make a break from the day's shopping. Maps are available at the trailhead.

The Ridge Trail is the longest path through the sanctuary, looping through the property with a little help from a service road. The 1.6-mile circuit leaves from the parking area heading northwest and enters the woods. The Orchard Trail soon enters from the right, but continue on the Ridge Trail and pass through the pines and an old orchard. Forest gives way to field and eventually you pass evidence of days gone by—a stone wall. Just on the other side of the wall is the Link Trail, which provides passage to the 0.5-mile Deer Run Trail. After the stone wall, the trail rises up gradually on a ridge surrounded by evergreens.

Nearly 0.5 mile into the trail, you reach the Larch Spur Trail. The dead-end trail leads to a bench under the canopy of trees. The Ridge Trail continues turning southeast, eventually passing the Deer Run Trail and a telephone company right-of-way.

The Bench Loop, a short 0.25-mile spur circuit, is a pleasant undertaking. Under the cover of trees, a bench waits for you. Enjoy the wooded views in the quiet of the forest.

Directions at a glance

0.0 Leave from parking area via the Ridge Trail heading northwest.

0.5 Pass Larch Spur Trail.

1.2 Turn right by the field and pass buildings.

1.4 Pass dam and continue on service road back to parking area.

Continuing on the Ridge Trail, the Day Camp building and Mill Master's House will come into view by an open field. During the summer, nature programs are held here. An option is to make a right on the Mill Stream Trail and follow it 0.3 mile as it winds along a stream bank, eventually leading back to the Ridge Trail.

Back on the Ridge Trail, you reach the old mill dam on the Harraseeket River Estuary. The mill provides a glimpse into history. The area was once a spot where ships were made, thus the name Mast Landing. The lumber and gristmills were active from the early 1700s until 1861, when the mill burned. Explore the huge stones.

The Ridge Trail continues along the service road that you pick up by the mill master's house, turning northwest again, and crosses the water. Just before the parking area, the Estuary Trail leaves to the left. It's a 0.4-mile trail to the river's edge and loops back to the service road. There is a bench for rest and reflection.

How to get there

From Freeport, leave Main Street and turn onto Bow Street, in front of L. L. Bean. Drive 1.0 mile and turn left on Upper Mast Landing Road. At 0.1 mile, follow the sign for the Mast Landing Sanctuary.

Piazza Rock

Appalachian Trail, Sandy River Plantation, Maine

Type of trail:	🌑
Also used by:	Hikers
Distance:	3.6 miles round-trip
Terrain:	Relatively flat with a couple of steep pitches to a huge, towering flat-topped boulder along the Appalachian Trail
Trail difficulty:	More difficult
Surface quality:	Unpacked
Time:	3½ hours
Food and facilities:	Two lean-tos and a toilet are located near Piazza Rock. The lean-tos are open year-round and are free. Top off water bottles before heading out. In Farmington, a town with a University of Maine campus, supplies, lodging, and food are plentiful. A Shop 'n Save is on Route 4. Aardvark Outfitters (207–778–3330) and Red Oak Sports (207–778–5350) have rentals. The Mount Blue Motel (207–778–6004) is on Route 4.
	If you are coming from Rangeley, Main Street is where you'll find what you need. Ski and snowshoe rentals can be had at the Alpine Shop (800–310–3741 or 207–864–3741). After the trek, head to the Red Onion, Main Street, for a sandwich or pizza (207–864–5022). For overnights, choose from among the fifty rooms at the Rangeley Inn, 51 Main Street (800–MOMENTS or 207–864–3341).
Phone numbers:	The Rangeley Chamber of Commerce can be reached at 207–864–5571 or 800–MT–LAKES.

What makes a good snowshoe trail? The answer is fairly simple: a reward for the effort. Outdoor prizes vary. Mountain, lake, and pond vistas are always worth the price of admission. Frozen waterfalls can be spectacular. Knowledge provides the impetus for a good outing, too. If a trail is rich in history, that can sometime add to the experience. Warming huts, fire towers, and shelters can also be focal points. Then again, there's nothing like the solitude found on any trail in the stillness of winter.

For those snowshoeing to Piazza Rock, the answer is in seeing an unusual natural phenomenon.

And a cribbage board in a two-holer.

Piazza Rock, a monolithic rock that seems to defy gravity and logic, is located at the end of short and fairly easy section of the Appalachian

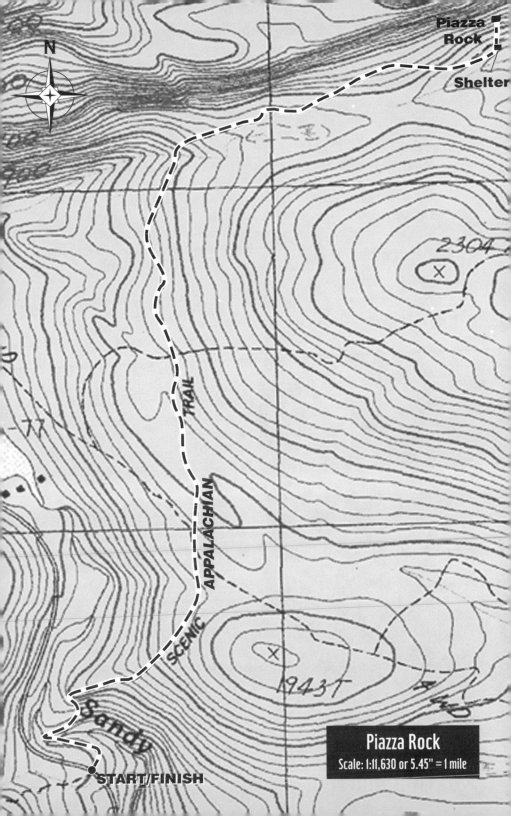

N

2304
X

TRAIL

APPALACHIAN

SCENIC

1943T
X

Sandy

START/FINISH

Piazza
Rock

Shelter

Piazza Rock
Scale: 1:11,630 or 5.45" = 1 mile

Trail, south of wild Rangeley Lake. The huge, flat, overhanging boulder invites exploration.

The trail is really quite easy, with the exception of two steep pitches at the beginning and end. Those two stretches bump the trail up into the more difficult category. There are also a handful of bridge crossings to negotiate.

The Appalachian Trail (AT) leaves the east side of Route 4 and gently heads down through the forest to the frozen Sandy River, where you encounter your first bridge crossing. Stop to admire the masonry of the flat boulders used for construction. On the other side of the river, the trail takes a hard left and begins to climb out of the valley. A sign detailing the AT is posted on a tree. The AT is blazed in white. The blazes are high on the trees. Be cognizant of them, particularly during a fruitful snow year. A double blaze indicates a sharp change in direction. AT spur trails are blazed in blue.

This portion of the AT, called section 8, is 32.2 miles and leads up the western side of Saddleback Mountain. Piazza Rock is far short of Saddleback.

Depending on the amount of snow, you may be able to see the wooden staircase up the ridge. If so, stay to one side and continue the short but steep, winding climb to the crest of the hill, where it levels off a bit. This is the toughest part of the trail until the final 500 feet or so up to Piazza Rock.

Once the trail becomes flatter, look to the right for a spot that serves up views of a ridge line. It is one of the few dramatic views during this snowshoe trip. If you crossed the second foot bridge, you missed it.

The trail winds through the woods, occasionally dipping here

Portions of the Appalachian Trail make fine snowshoe outings in Maine during winter. The AT is blazed in white with spur trails marked in blue. Snowshoers can sign in at registration boxes.

and there. At mile 1.1, the trail crosses a logging road and reenters the woods on the other side. Short, new growth pine trees line the narrow trail before opening up into what looks like a gladed forest.

At 1.5 miles, a registration station comes into view. There are mileage markers and cards asking for comments about the trail for hikers to fill out . Just up ahead, in about 0.2 mile, are a signboard, the lean-to, and toilet. On the sign is a thermometer. Wondering how cold it is in the Maine woods? There's the answer.

The lean-to is a good lunch and rest spot. Afterward, turn left at the sign by the lean-to on the blue-blazed trail to begin the steep trek up to Piazza Rock. This lean-to, called the Piazza Rock Lean-to, was built by the Civilian Conservation Corps in 1935. There are large boulders in the area. They can be very icy, as can Piazza Rock. Sit under the rock. Try and climb on top of it. There aren't any stunning views from the top but you'll certainly get a unique perspective on the happenings down below.

From the Piazza Rock Lean-to, it's just about 150 feet or so to a second lean-to, constructed by the Maine Appalachian Trail Club in 1993. Cross the stream to a junction and turn right. The lean-to is there plus a two-hole privy, complete with cribbage board. Bring your own cards—and toilet paper too.

"It's the hot spot on the Maine section of the AT. Thru hikers [those who attempt to hike the entire Appalachian Trail] talk about it all the time," said Rob Tice, a caretaker at Piazza Rock in 1996.

Chances are, so will you.

Directions at a glance

0.0 Leave Route 4 on the white-blazed Appalachian Trail, following the sign pointing to Piazza Rock.

1.5 Pass registration box—or stop to fill out card.

1.7 Turn left near lean-to on blue-blazed trail to Piazza Rock.

1.8 Reach Piazza Rock. Return via the same trail.

1.9 Turn right on Appalachian Trail.

2.1 Pass registration box.

3.6 Reach Route 4.

How to get there

From the junction of Routes 2 and 4 in Farmington, follow Route 4 north for 32 miles to trailhead on the east side (right).

From the junction of Routes 4 and 16 in Rangeley, follow Route 4 south for 10 miles to the trailhead on the east side (left).

Parking is limited at the trailhead, which is just a plowed section of the roadside shoulder. The trail sign might be obscured by high snow-banks, but there is an Appalachian Trail sign and a large metal "A" on the west side of the road.

Bunawabskeg (Redington Pond) Loop
Sugarloaf/USA Outdoor Center, Carrabassett Valley, Maine

Type of trail: ➤ ◄ ▨

Distance: 6.1-mile loop

Terrain: Rolling, flat

Trail difficulty: Easiest

Surface quality: Tracked, skate groomed

Time: 2 hours skiing

Food and facilities: Rentals, retail shop, lessons, guided tours, cafeteria, and fireplace are all available at the base lodge of the Sugarloaf/USA Outdoor Center. The wax room is in a separate building. Ice skating (and rentals) are also offered. You can rent pulks. Trail passes are sold at the base lodge, plus at the base lodge at Sugarloaf and at the front desk of the Sugarloaf Inn. The Sugarloaf Inn (207–237–6814), on the road to Sugarloaf, is a comfortable place to stay. For a posttrip meal of hearty fare, try the burgers at the Bag (207–237–2451), located in the base village at Sugarloaf.

Phone numbers: Call the Sugarloaf/USA Outdoor Center at (207) 237–6830.

A jewel of a mountain, remote Sugarloaf is the second-highest mountain in Maine. Though the 'Loaf in winter is primarily associated with downhill skiing and snowboarding, the 60-mile network of cross-country ski trails at the Sugarloaf/USA Outdoor Center near the base of the pyramid-shaped mountain are groomed pathways through the Maine woods with views of the snow-capped Bigelow Range. With the explosion of snowshoeing, webbed trekkers can waddle on the skate lane of all 60 miles or twist their way through the 18 miles of snowshoe-only trails. One rigorous snowshoe trip is the 8.0-mile round-trip climb to the summit of Burnt Mountain via the East Trail. From the summit, the panorama includes the slopes of Sugarloaf, and if the clouds are taking the day off, distant Mount Washington in New Hampshire and wild Katahdin in Baxter State Park.

Billing itself as Maine's largest Nordic trail network, the system does see a lot of use from recreational and competitive skiers. Aside from special events, like moonlight tours, the center plays host to major races from Bill Koch events to Masters' levels. The network tends to open early (around Thanksgiving) and stay open late (maybe Easter). In addition to the natural snow, there is a small 2.0-mile loop that is serviced by snowmaking machines.

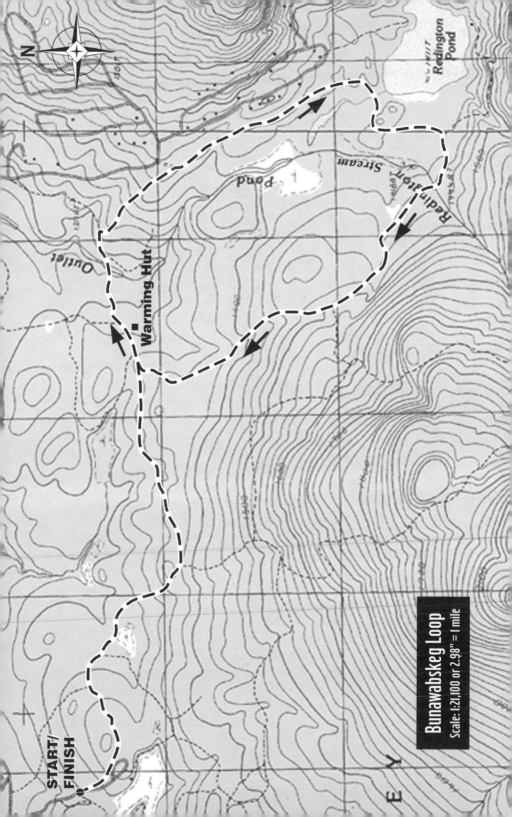

Redington
Pond

Stream

Redington

Pond

Outlet

Warming Hut

N

START/
FINISH

Bunawabskeg Loop
Scale: 1:21,100 or 2.98" = 1 mile

The trail network is a partnership of rather unique neighbors. The land is owned by the town of Carrabassett Valley, Maine's Bureau of Public Lands, Sugarloaf, and the Penobscot Indian Nation. Skiing the trails can also be a foreign language lesson because its names are Penobscot words. This loop utilizes three of the trails: *Bunawabskeg* means Penobscot, *Seeboosis* is small river, *Damakguay* is beaver.

The trails along the golf course, like Seewanhee (trail 1), are wide open and offer Bigelow Range vistas. Another slide on the easy side is the 6.0-mile-long Woodabogan (trail 9), which follows the old narrow gauge railroad bed from Bigelow Station in the north to Houston Brook Road in the valley. On weekends and holidays, a shuttle bus ferries skiers who want to do only a portion of the ski. Dogs are allowed on that trail. Serious skiers looking for a strenuous workout should add Geesoos (trail 50) to their list of trails to conquer.

Looking like a white desert, the frozen waters of Redington Pond at the Sugarloaf Outdoor Skiing Center are a quiet place to reflect or to look for wildlife.

The Bunawabskeg, or Redington Pond, Loop weaves through the wooded lowlands, by cedars, over bridges that span small streams, and by a warming hut, a necessary place to visit during deep winter cold. A star spot on the loop is the very short-side trail to the still and frozen shores of Redington Pond. A smartly placed picnic table by the shores encourages quiet reflection during the sunny days of winter. The signs on the loop are well-placed, but there are no maps posted at key interesections saying "You are here" to help those who are unfamiliar with the area.

The loop begins outside the base lodge, which has got an incredible view of the mountain. You'll follow wide Seeboosis only for a brief spell before getting on the twisting Damakguay. Follow the trail past the Pretty Bog vista, which looks south to the alpine slopes. At the bog, the trail joins a logging road and rises moderately to a warming hut. Shortly, Bunawabskeg becomes the main thoroughfare for the loop in the eastern part of the network. Bunawabskeg is flat for about a 0.5 mile before it gradually ascends. You pass a Penobscot Indian Nation hunting cabin just before reaching the side trail to Redington Pond (about 3.3 miles from the base lodge). The pond is ringed by the ridgeline of Burnt and Sugarloaf Mountains. Roll through mixed hardwoods on Bunawabskeg and enjoy a downhill before rejoining Damakguay. Near the tops of the trees, look for the northern vistas out to the Bigelows before rolling back to the base lodge.

Directions at a glance

0.0 Leave the lodge on Seeboosis (trail 1), going south.

0.1 Bear left on Damakguay (trail 5).

1.5 Bear left on Bunawabskeg (trail 8).

4.5 Turn left on Damakguay (trail 5).

6.0 Turn left on Seeboosis (trail 1).

How to get there

From the junctions of Routes 27, 16, and 142 in Kingfield, take Route 27 north for 14.7 miles and turn left at the sign for the Suglarloaf/USA Outdoor Center. From Sugarloaf, turn right on Route 27 and travel about 1.0 mile before making a right at the sign for the Sugarloaf/USA Outdoor Center.

Bald Mountain Trail
Oquossoc, Maine

Type of trail:	⬤⬤⬤
Also used by:	Hikers, snowmobilers (portions)
Distance:	2.0 miles round-trip
Terrain:	The lake views into Rangeley and beyond make the hilly climb worthwhile
Trail difficulty:	More difficult
Surface quality:	Unpacked
Time:	2 hours
Food and facilities:	Snowshoe rentals are available in nearby Rangeley at the Alpine Shop, 72 Main Street (800–310–3741 or 207–864–3741). The Carry Road Country Store (207–864–3662) on Route 4 in Oquossoc has groceries and a deli. In Rangeley, Mike's Sports Pub and Grub (207–864–5616) on Main Street has a number of specials to choose from. Rangeley has a number of overnight accommodations; in Oquossoc there is River's Edge Cottage on Route 4 (207–864–5582).
Phone numbers:	The Rangeley Chamber of Commerce has information on the area and can be reached at 207–864–5571. Maine's Bureau of Parks and Land, P. O. Box 327, Farmington, Maine 04938 (207–778–4111) is a good contact, too.

They say that location is everything. That's why Bald Mountain is a small mountain that hands out a big adventure. The 2,443-foot mountain is on some prime public real estate, sandwiched between Rangeley and Mooselookmeguntic Lakes near the active village of Oquossoc. Bald Mountain is a bit of a misleading name. At one time, a fire tower graced the summit, but it is now gone. There was also a time when the bedrock summit may have afforded spectacular treeless views of the lakes and mountains. Whatever tonic Bald Mountain uses, it's working. The woods have grown up, though in winter, with the leaves gone, you can saunter out on a ledge and be rewarded with a bird's-eye look at the land below. Another added bonus is a very short spur trail about three-quarters of the way up that leads to a scramble atop a ledge, allowing you a look at the frozen landscape below.

The blue-blazed Bald Mountain Trail is a hiking trail in summer. Initially, it is easy to follow. As the snowshoe trek reaches the evergreen summit, the trail steepens and twists to the bald summit, where a picnic

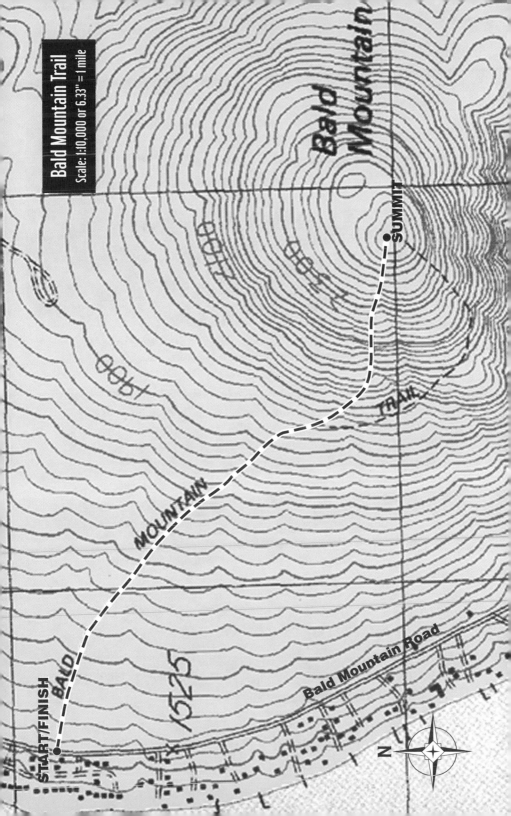

Bald Mountain Trail
Scale: 1:10,000 or 6.33" = 1mile

Bald Mountain

SUMMIT

1400

1600

1700

1200

BALD MOUNTAIN TRAIL

1525

Bald Mountain Road

START/FINISH

N

A snowshoe trip up the Bald Mountain Trail in Oquossoc, Maine, leads to rewarding views of Rangeley and Mooselookmeguntic Lakes.

table is perched. In winter, the village of Oquossoc maintains a snow-mobile trail that goes over the mountain as well. The hiking trail and the snowmobile trail are one and the same for the first 0.5 mile or so, before the hiking trail takes a hard right and heads off on its own.

The trail, maintained by the state, leaves from the parking area on a gradual wide ascent through the hardwood forest. A short distance from the start, it branches. Stay left and follow the blue blazes. The gentle grade continues as the path jogs hard right, but then changes its disposition as it starts to climb a bit steeply up to the pines. The trail will narrow and the pitches will become more challenging. Be sure to look through the trees down below.

Near the 0.75-mile mark, take the spur trail to the left; it goes maybe 50 feet to a ledge with awe-inspiring vistas. The scramble to the top could be icy depending on the amount of snowfall. The Bald Mountain Trail continues upward, finally reaching

Directions at a glance

0.0 Leave the trailhead heading east on the Bald Mountain Trail.

0.5 Blue-blazed trail bears hard right.

0.75 Scenic overlook is on left

1.0 Reach summit. Return via Bald Mountain Trail.

1.5 Trail bears hard left.

2.0 Reach parking area and trailhead.

the summit with its picnic table. Carefully mosey out to the open ledges for uninterrupted views. On the north side of the mountain, there is a communications tower and the grown-over trails from a long dormant ski area.

How to get there

In Oquossoc, travel on Route 4 north for 1.1 mile to Bald Mountain Road. Turn left on Bald Mountain Road and travel 0.8 mile to the parking area and trailhead on the left. If it is unplowed, park by the roadside.

Burnham Hill Loop

Rangeley Municipal Trails, Rangeley, Maine

Type of trail:	▬ , ◄ , ▧ (portions)
Distance:	7.4-mile loop
Terrain:	Gentle, rolling, and steep
Trail difficulty:	Yellow and Green Loops range from easiest to more difficult; Blue Loop, most difficult
Surface quality:	Tracked, skate-groomed
Time:	2½ hours
Food and facilities:	Facilities on this network are spartan. No water or rest rooms are available, but there is a warming hut with wood-stove on the Burnham Hill Loop. Trail passes may be obtained at the trail hut off Route 4, the Rangeley Chamber of Commerce office at 1 Park Road, off Main Street, and at the Alpine Shop, 72 Main Street (800–310–3741 or 207–864–3741). Ski and snowshoe rentals can be had at the Alpine Shop. After the trek, head to the Red Onion, Main Street, for a sandwich or pizza (207–864–5022). For overnights, choose from the fifty rooms at the Rangeley Inn, 51 Main Street (800–MOMENTS or 207–864–3341).
Phone numbers:	The Rangeley Chamber of Commerce has information on the trail system and can be reached at (207) 864–5571 or (800) MT–LAKES.

Moose in the roads and moose mounted on walls are intertwined with the rugged and brawny character of Rangeley. This western Maine community is the gateway to winter recreation. Though snowmobilers are the dominant force on the trails, skiers and snowshoers can find trail systems to play on as well. Some 15 miles of groomed trails are located at the base of the Saddleback Ski Area, about 7 miles from town. But down in Rangeley,

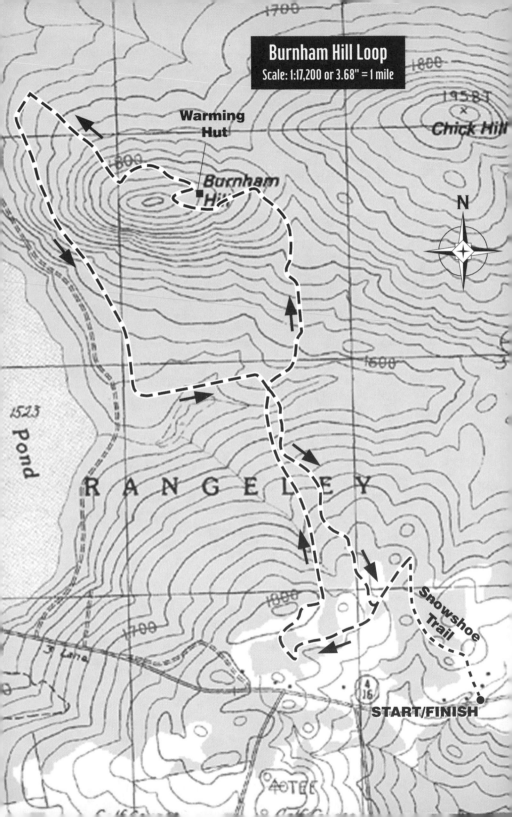

the mushrooming volunteerism of a core of about thirty diehard cross-country skiers has led to the development of some 15 miles of trails called Rangeley Municipal Trails. As snowmobling grew in the area, skiers began looking for their own trails to ski. In 1989, a group of skiers made a small out-and-back trail on land off Route 16. From there, they approached the town about using some property near the town's transfer station. They groomed a small 1.0-mile loop that came to be known as the Two Moose Trail, just because someone saw a couple of moose out there one time. Serendipity also played a role in the system's development. When the town started to develop Chick Hill for a sewer treatment plant, an area that has wide panoramic views of Saddleback and the Bigelows, the network expanded to that land as well.

At one time, the warming hut on Rangeley Municipal Trails was on the verge of collapse. A group of local skiers pooled their resources and rebuilt the hut, which now has a woodstove, couch, and chairs.

As time progressed, the group, the nonprofit Rangeley Cross-Country Ski Club, raised money through their fund-raising efforts and grant writing. The skiers contacted various landowners, and what once was just an out-and-back trail is now a network run by volunteers. At one time, the network was run on a donation basis. In the winter of 1998-99, a small fee was established.

More trails are planned for the future, including a 7.0-mile trail with panoramas of Spotted Mountain. Facilities along the network are spartan; there are just a small ticket booth and a warming hut on the Burnham Hill Loop. If all goes well, another warming hut will be built.

The trails are nicely groomed and utilize a color-coded system for navigation. Trail names have been replaced by colors. There are four loops, dubbed Blue, Red, Yellow, and Green Loops. Follow the color and you'll be all set. Trail system maps with locator dots are conveniently placed at intersections.

When it comes to snowshoes, the volunteers have come up with an interesting spin. As of 1998-99, snowshoes are only allowed on the 3.0-mile Yellow Loop and only if the temperature is under 28 degrees F. Why? Groomers found it difficult to track over the frozen snowshoe prints.

Rangeley can get downright cold. Though the 2.0-mile Red Loop over Chick Hill serves up the vistas, it should only be tackled on those calm, sunny winter days. Other days, stick to the wooded trails.

The Blue Loop, or Burnham Hill Loop, is a 3.2-mile thriller with three dizzying switchbacks through the hardwoods and views of the frozen Dodge Pond and surrounding peaks. Better skiers should try the loop, while beginners and intermediates can use the rest of the network.

The big loop, utilizing Yellow, Green, and Blue Trails, begins from the ticket hut off Route 4 on the Yellow Trail, which crosses open fields with ridgelines popping up in the distance. Yellow leads into the pine forest, which provides shelter from the wind, if Old Man Winter is blowing hard. The trail is relatively flat before handing off to Green, a pleasant 1.0-mile-long winding descent through the woods on a more difficult path. Don't get too relaxed. The work is

Directions at a glance

0.0 Leave the hut from the Route 4 trailhead on the Yellow Trail, heading north.

0.2 Turn left on Yellow Trail at junction with unsigned trail.

0.4 Turn left on Yellow Trail and ski about 100 feet.

0.4 Turn left on Yellow Trail, ski about 100 feet, then turn left on Yellow/Green Trail.

0.6 Turn right on Green Trail.

1.6 Turn right onto Blue Trail.

2.6 Reach the warming hut. Continue on Blue Trail.

4.8 Turn right for Yellow Trail and gradual climb. Watch for powerlines.

6.8 Bear right on Yellow/Green.

7.0 Turn right on Yellow and ski about 100 feet.

7.0 Turn left on Yellow.

7.2 Turn left to parking area.

about to begin. The Blue Trail begins a 1.0-mile-long grunt through the hardwoods to the warming hut. The warming hut is also a testament to the volunteers. The hut was in disrepair. Volunteers fixed it up for less than $500 (and managed to clean out some little used furniture in their homes) and came up with a cozy cabin in the woods. If you use the woodstove, be sure to replace the wood you use from the pile outside.

Now the trail gets interesting. Three steep switchbacks provide thrilling pitches before the trail mellows out along power lines, which are adjacent to the trail. Blue leads to Yellow and one more long, gradual climb. The Yellow Trail wiggles along and comes out into the open, providing views of the ski trails at Saddleback and the snow-packed Bigelows. Dip back into the woods over some familiar territory before the last jaunt through the open fields to the parking area.

How to get there

From Rangeley, travel on Route 4 west for 1.7 miles and turn right at the sign, showing a cross-country skier, for Rangeley Municipal Trails.

Table Rock

Grafton Notch State Park, Grafton Notch, Maine

Type of trail:	⬤
Also used by:	Winter hikers
Distance:	2.8 miles round-trip
Terrain:	Gradual ascent with a couple of switchbacks to ledge overlooking Grafton Notch
Trail difficulty:	Easiest
Surface quality:	Unpacked
Time:	3 hours
Food and facilities:	Toilets are available at the trailhead, but there is no drinking water. Nearby Bethel and Newry have convenience stores for last minute items; the area is home to a number of cross-country ski centers and two downhill ski areas. After your tour you'll find the Sunday River Brewing Company (207–824–4253) quite lively. It's on Sunday River Road in Bethel. Snowshoes and cross-country ski rentals are available from the ski shops at both the Sunday River (207–824–2410) and Bethel Inn (207–824–6276) trail systems. Various accommodations are available in the area, such as the Androscoggin Valley Motel, Route 2, West Bethel (207–836–3611).
Phone numbers:	Information on Grafton Notch State Park may be had by writing Grafton Notch State Park, HCR 61, P. O. Box 330, Newry, Maine 04261. The phone number (not in use during winter) is (207) 824–2912. Information may also be had by contacting the Maine Department of Conservation at (207) 287–3821.

Table Rock is a perch from which one can gaze upon winter's glory. Nearly 1,000 feet above one of Maine's most scenic roads, the massive flattened ledge is an alfresco table smack across from the state's third-

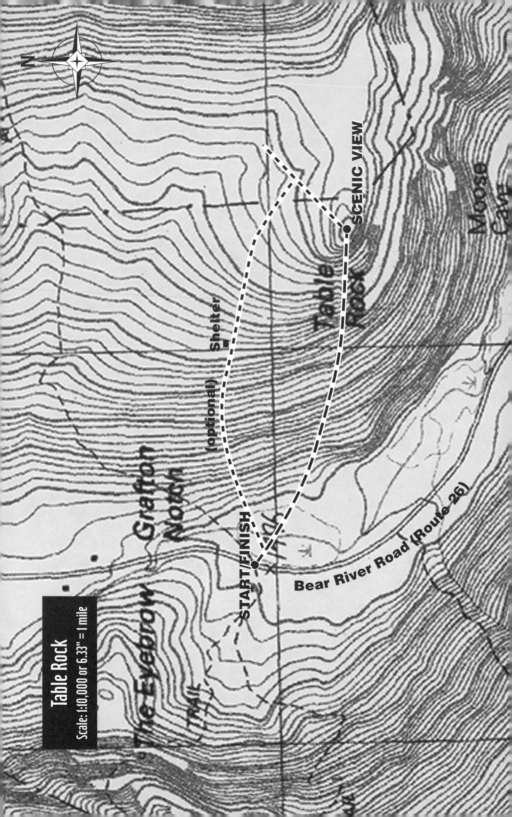

highest peak—Old Speck. Ranked behind Katahdin and Sugarloaf, Old Speck stands at an impressive 4,180 feet. From Table Rock, look across at the mountain down into the undulating hills through the notch.

The huge ledge (visible from the highway at the Moose Cave parking area) is part of the 3,192-acre Grafton Notch State Park. The park is ripe with hiking trails and wildlife. To climb Old Speck in winter is quite an undertaking. To snowshoe to Table Rock via the Appalachian Trail (AT) is to attain maximum views for nominal efforts. The Appalachian Trail runs roughly 2,000 miles from Georgia to Maine. The Maine section includes mountains like Old Speck and Baldplate. Snowshoers who follow this route to Table Rock should know they are walking in the foot-

steps of intrepid thru hikers, people who travel the entire length of the rigorous trail. A few notices near the trailhead tell hikers about the AT in Maine. There may even be handwritten advertisements covered in plastic and tacked to a birch telling thru hikers of overnight accommodations in the towns that lay ahead in the north.

Table Rock, about 900 feet above the valley floor, is an open ledge.

Table Rock, in Grafton Notch, is a ledge outcrop that affords fine views. The sign along the trail isn't lying.

Use caution while out on the plateau. Though this snowshoe to the outcrop is fairly easy, it is not a good trip for small children. There are other opportunities in Grafton Notch for them. Children can flop around in their snowshoes in the picnic area by Screw Auger Falls. The 0.25-mile loop by Moose Cave provides a pleasant walk (leave the snowshoes behind). Just watch your footing on the steps. Actually, if you've got some zip left after Table Rock, stop at those two areas on the way out of the park. Screw Auger Falls has huge boulders and pools, while Moose Cave is a deep and narrow flume, covered with icicles. Legend has it that a hunter heard a moose trapped in a cave. Instead of offering help, he killed the moose and served up Bullwinkle on the dinner table.

The Appalachian Trail leaves the trailhead, crosses the road, and enters the woods by a marshy area with log bridges. Soon thereafter, the trail passes by a junction with the Table Rock Trail, which leaves to the right. During the nonsnow months, the Table Rock Trail is a steep, boulder-strewn path to Table Rock. Thinking about snowshoeing on it? Forget about it. Stay to the left.

The AT, which leads to Baldplate Mountain, is a moderate ascent up through the hardwoods. At about 0.4 mile, the trail takes a hard right and goes through a series of brief switchbacks and a couple of easy stream crossings. At about 0.7 mile into the journey, the trail takes another hard right and widens as it becomes an old woods road. The path follows along a stream and soon diverges from the AT.

The AT swings to the left at the 0.9-mile mark. At that junction, a sign points to Table Rock and promises extraordinary views. It isn't lying. Turn right on the blue-blazed Upper Table Rock Trail. The trail gently ascends for just over 0.4 mile. The final pitch to Table Rock is a quick, steep push to the pines. The orange-blazed Table Rock Trail will enter from the left (about 1.4 miles into the route). Head straight through the pines about 20 yards to the horizontal shelf. Pat yourself on the back for a job well done before returning to the parking area along the same route.

Directions at a glance

0.0 Leave the parking area, taking the white-blazed Appalachian Trail (the trail on the right) east and cross Route 26.

0.1 Turn left at junction with Table Rock Trail (blazed orange). Stay left and follow white-blazed Appalachian Trail.

0.9 Turn right on blue-blazed Upper Table Rock Trail.

1.4 Orange-blazed Table Rock Trail enters left. Stay straight on the blue-blazed trail for a few more feet to Table Rock and views. Return to parking area via the same route.

How to get there

From Bethel, take Route 2 east about 8 miles to junction with Route 26 north (Bear River Road). Turn left on Route 26 and travel to Grafton Notch State Park. The, trailhead, which is on the left side of the road, is 12.5 miles from the junction of Routes 2 and 26. A sign says HIKING TRAILS. The trailhead is between the towns of Newry and Upton. Route 26 is quite scenic and offers opportunities to stop at other attractive places, like Screw Auger Falls and Moose Cave.

Corkscrew Loop
Bethel Inn and Country Club, Bethel, Maine

Type of trail:	▬▬ ◄ ⬤
Distance:	5-mile loop
Terrain:	Flat, rolling, and challenging—all mixed together for a corker of a ski
Trail difficulty:	Most difficult
Surface quality:	Groomed and tracked
Time:	2 hours skiing
Food and facilities:	Rentals for skiers and snowshoers are available at the Bethel Inn and Country Club's Nordic Center ski shop. Pulks can be rented too. Lessons, light snacks, toilet facilities, and water are also offered. The inn is also the site of numerous special events during the winter. The inn itself is an elegant country property with fine dining. Guests receive trail passes as part of their overnight stay. There is a trail fee for nonguests. The Millbrook Tavern, located in the inn, has hearty fare for a postski meal.
Phone numbers:	The Bethel Inn and Country Club's Nordic Center can be reached at (207) 824–6276. The inn's number is (800) 654–0125. For information on cross-country skiing in Bethel, call the Maine Nordic Ski Council at (207) 824–3694.

Bethel is home to four cross-country ski areas, serving up miles of varied terrain along rivers, on valley floors, and into hills. Throw in the groomed trails of the local high school, Telstar, and a boarding school known for its ski programs, Gould Academy, and you've got a healthy mix. The two schools, which have ski teams, have more challenging terrain to better suit the student athletes. Still, in Bethel skiers and snowshoers can choose from the trails at Carter's, the Sunday River Inn, Telemark Inn (reservations a must), and the Bethel Inn and Country Club.

For anyone who has walked the streets of Bethel to the Common, the Bethel Inn is a remembered landmark. The regal yellow clapboard structure is a focal point in this town, which was founded in 1796. Dr. John George Gehring came to Bethel after practicing surgery in his native Cleveland, where he suffered mental and physical breakdowns. The mountains of western Maine were soothing compared with frenetic city life, even in the late 1800s. Dr. Gehring returned to practicing medicine in 1895, treating nervous disorders with therapy that included healthy outdoor activites. In 1913, he and five patients, entered into a partnership

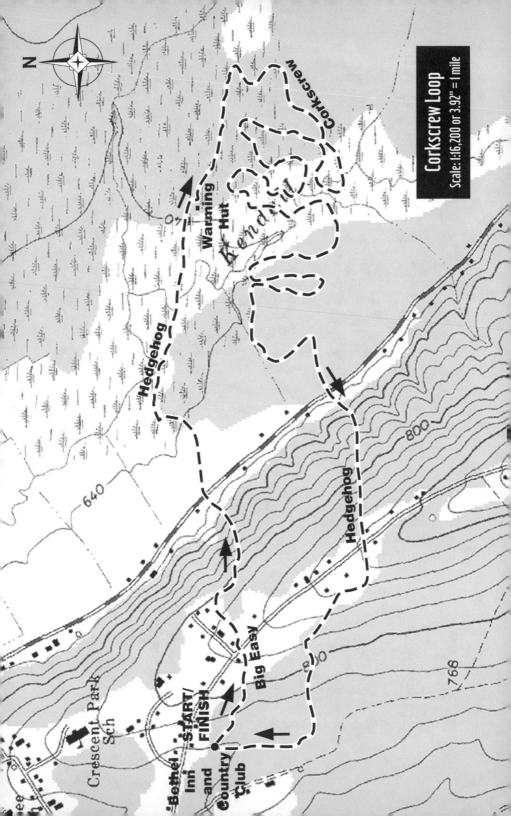

Corkscrew Loop
Scale: 1:16,200 or 3.92" = 1 mile

Corkscrew

Warming Hut

Glendale

Hedgehog

Hedgehog

Big Easy

800

800

768

640

START/FINISH

Crescent Park Sch

Bethel Inn and Country Club

N

to build the inn, which stands today. Interestingly, there are about 2,300 residents in Bethel, while the inn hosts some 35,000 guests per year.

The inn is the centerpiece of a groomed trail network that offers 20 miles of skiing and snowshoeing. Snowshoers are allowed on all of the network's trails, and also enjoy about 5 miles of ungroomed but marked trails all to themselves.

In the winter of 1973–74, the cross-country ski network began operation. About 20 percent of the trails are on the golf course, with the rest allowing exploration into the mixed hardwood forests, offering glimpses of Baldpate, Old Speck, and Caribou-Speckled Mountains. You'll spot deer, moose, and hares—or at least their tracks. For beginners, the Big Easy is the loop to do. It's about 3.0 miles of rolling terrain that ducks into the woods. Hedghog is another easy loop. Intermediate skiers and snowshoers will like Paradise Trail. But, better skiers can use Big Easy and Hedgehog as paths to one of the most most exhilarating groomed skis in the area—Corkscrew.

Corkscrew was once a series of unconnected trails. But under the direction of the tour center's director, Steve Jackson, they were cut together for a hair-raising rollercoaster ride over bridges, swooping through dips and climbing a few hills. A warming hut, just before the winding trail, is a good spot to drink in the views before putting that cardiovascular system to work.

With a mountainous backdrop, skiers of all abilities can explore the many miles of trails at the Bethel Inn's touring center.

Experience the Corkscrew by first warming up on the easy glide along the golf course via the Big Easy. The inn is the backdrop as the wide trail heads down and rolls across the open course. Hedgehog is a relatively flat grade and leads into the woods. When it takes a hard ninety-degree turn to the right, look for the warming hut and prepare to twist and shout through the pine. The trail winds around several bridges and stream crossings. All it takes is a few minutes of skiing or snowshoeing to see how this trail got its name. Some 2.5 miles into the total trip, cross Hedgehog again and swoop down and up by a stream. The part of Corkscrew, just before it connects with Hedgehog, is called "the tail" and whips out onto the golf course for some winter mountain views. Hedghog reenters the woods on a gentle, wide, 2 or 3 percent grade down to the golf course before the final short climb back to the inn.

Directions at a glance

0.0   Leave by the touring center sign, taking the Big Easy trail down and to the left across the open golf course.

0.6   Turn right onto Hedgehog and around 1.0 mile start looking for the warming hut.

1.2   Turn left on Corkscrew.

1.5   Bear right on Corkscrew as it intersects with Moose.

3.25 Bear left on Corkscrew

3.5   Turn right on Hedgehog and follow it 1.5 miles back to the touring center.

How to get there

Route 26 in Bethel becomes Main Street. Follow Main Street to the Common where it intersects with Church and Broad Streets. The inn is located there.

Farwell Mountain Loop

Carter's Cross-Country Ski Center, Bethel, Maine

Type of trail: ▬ ◄ ●

Distance: 5.0-mile-loop; optional Field Loop 4.0 miles

Terrain: From Farwell Mountain, look across to the Mahoosucs and Presidentials, but be prepared to work that heart to get there.

Trail difficulty: Most difficult

Surface quality: Groomed

Time: 2 hours

Food and facilities: Carter's Cross-Country Ski Center has a ski shop, snowshoe and ski rentals, lessons, water, and rest rooms. It has snacks, too. Snowshoers are allowed on all trails. For overnights, Carter's has two lodges, a mountain cabin, and yurt. Hungry afterward? Try Finish Line Pizza on Main Street in Bethel.

Phone numbers: Carter's Cross-Country Ski Center is (207) 539–4848.

From the picnic table at the scenic overlook on a flat spot on Farwell Mountain, life can be grand. Out in the distance, the Mahoosuc and Presidential Ranges stand at attention. Mount Washington, the Carter-Moriahs, Sunday River Ski Area, Mt. Will, and even Old Speck line the horizon. This is one of the finest views in the Bethel area.

But you have to work to get there.

The Scenic Overlook, as it's called at Carter's, is fairly well known. With the introduction in the winter of 1998–99 of a new long, steep trail called Dick's Dive, advanced skiers who like challenges will earn those views.

From a picnic table at the height of land at Carter's in Bethel, skiers rest with scenic vistas as a backdrop.

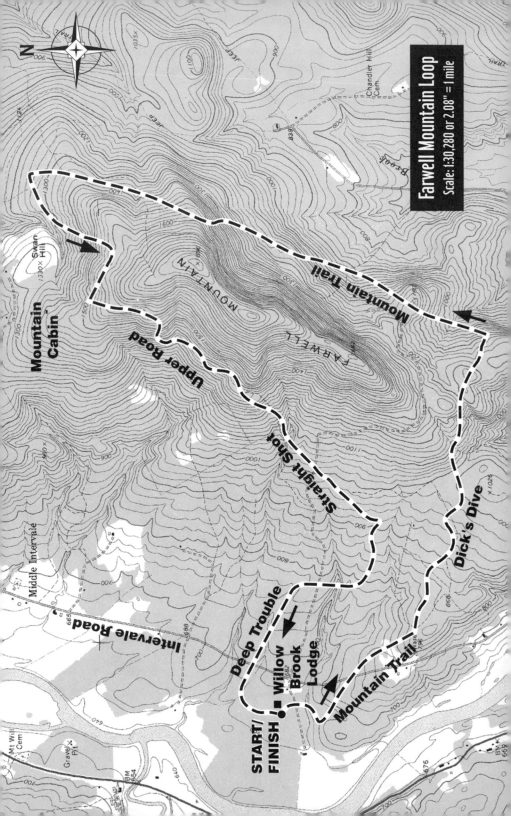

Farwell Mountain Loop
Scale: 1:30,280 or 2.08" = 1 mile

David Carter runs Carter's Cross-Country Ski Center in Bethel and the one in Oxford, just about 35 miles outside Portland, too. The Oxford trail system came first. Carter, a one-time ski racer who competed at high school, college, and post-college levels for a decade, also helped organize and run a couple of New Hampshire ski areas before opening the Oxford trails in 1981, then the Bethel system in 1991. The Oxford network has about 25 miles of trails, largely suited for the beginner and intermediate skier. The trails have views of the Little Androscoggin River, a couple of ponds, and a bog.

The mountains of Bethel make that terrain very interesting. Skiers of all abilities will find something on the 40 miles of trails (there's more if you count the adjacent backcountry and snowmobile trails). Beginners usually stick to the northern side of Carter's, staying on the trails outside the Willow Brook Lodge. From the wooded trails, like the River Trail, it is a little more than 1 mile down to the Androscoggin River and a nearby yurt, where day-trippers can rest and overnighters can stay. The 4.0-mile flat Field Loop encircles an area that has the old Carter homestead and old church.

The southern side of the network has a mountain cabin and lots of hills. Dick's Dive is recommended for advanced skiers only. For those who consider themselves just below that level, consider taking the Straight Shot Mountain Trail segment of this loop to the Scenic Overlook as an out-and-back adventure.

The Farwell Mountain Loop begins on the trail on the southern side of Intervale Road, marked by a Mountain Trail sign. The trail begins on a flat note and passes a farmhouse before entering the pines. Dick's Dive is signed. Now the 1.0-mile-long, steep climb starts. At first, the trail goes up through the evergreens with unforgiving pitches. The trail mellows out a bit as it passes from the forest to an open area that has been cut. Turn around for those mountain vistas. At the junction with Scenic Overlook, turn right on the very wide thoroughfare. Skaters will like it here because the trail is flat for a spell. The vistas are beautiful—the trail

Directions at a glance

0.0 Leave the lodge going southwest on Mountain Trail, which leads to Dick's Dive.

1.5 Turn right onto Scenic Overlook.

2.5 Reach Scenic Overlook picnic table.

3.1 Return to junction with Mountain Trail via Scenic Overlook. Stay straight on Mountain Trail.

4.3 Turn left on Upper Road.

4.6 Go straight on Straight Shot.

4.8 Turn right on Deep Trouble and return 0.3 miles to the touring center.

winds a bit before passing through a gate and heading upward. Snake around by a wooden home and land at a picnic table. That's about 2.5 miles. Catch your breath and play "name the peaks."

Return by the same route to the junction with Dick's Dive. The intrepid skier can turn left and dive down. That's a personal choice. Otherwise, stay straight back on Mountain Trail and wind down, looking out to Grafton Notch and Old Speck. Mountain Trail bears to the left and then serves up a choice: Upper Road or Sidewinder. Both are raucous roller-coaster rides through the woods. Go left on Upper Road to Straight Shot (Sidewinder goes there too) before merging to the right onto Deep Trouble, which drops back to Intervale Road.

Take off the skis to cross the road. Then gently slide back to the lodge.

How to get there
From Bethel, travel on Route 2 to Route 26 south. Turn left onto Intervale Road and drive about 3.5 miles to Carter's, which is on the left.

Artist's Covered Bridge Loop
Sunday River Inn and Cross-Country Ski Center, Bethel, Maine

Type of trail:	═══ ◄
Distance:	4.5-mile loop
Terrain:	Flat to rolling ski to a quintessential Maine covered bridge
Trail difficulty:	Easiest
Surface quality:	Tracked, skate groomed
Time:	2 hours
Food and facilities:	A full-service ski shop awaits visitors at the Sunday River Cross-Country Ski Center, complete with ski and snowshoe rentals. Kick sleds and pulks are also available for rent. Lessons are offered. Special events are held. Rest rooms, water, light snacks, and toilet facilities are located in the Nordic Center. Overnight accommodations can be had at the adjacent Sunday River Inn; a trail pass is included in the lodging fee. Sud's Pub (207–824–6558) on Main Street in nearby Bethel is a fun place for an après-ski pizza.
Phone numbers:	The Sunday River Inn and Cross-Country Ski Center can be reached by calling (207) 824–2410.

The setting is classic New England: Ski through the quiet and shelter of a snow-laden old-growth pine forest. Come upon a clearing where a weather-beaten covered bridge spans a frigid rushing river.

The scene is real, and you can find it on the Artist's Covered Bridge Loop at the Sunday River Inn and Cross-Country Ski Center.

The handsome bridge, constructed in 1872, is said to be the most photographed and painted in Maine. The Sunday River Valley was a summer retreat for urban artists from New York and Boston from the 1880s to the early 1900s, when trains transported the flock to Bethel. Staying in area boarding houses, painters used the bridge as inspiration. It was given its fifteen minutes of fame in a John Enneking painting.

Bethel and Newry are once again retreats, now in winter too, with the birth and growth of the Sunday River resort. Eight interconnected mountain peaks attract skiers and snowboarders by the carload, and the development of the resort has had a rippling effect on the surrounding area. Nordic skiers will find about 25 miles of trails at the Sunday River Inn and Cross Country Ski Center, located about a mile from the ski resort. Opened in 1972, the center has about 5 miles of its terrain open to snowshoers. The Barker Brook Loop is a short, fun and scenic romp

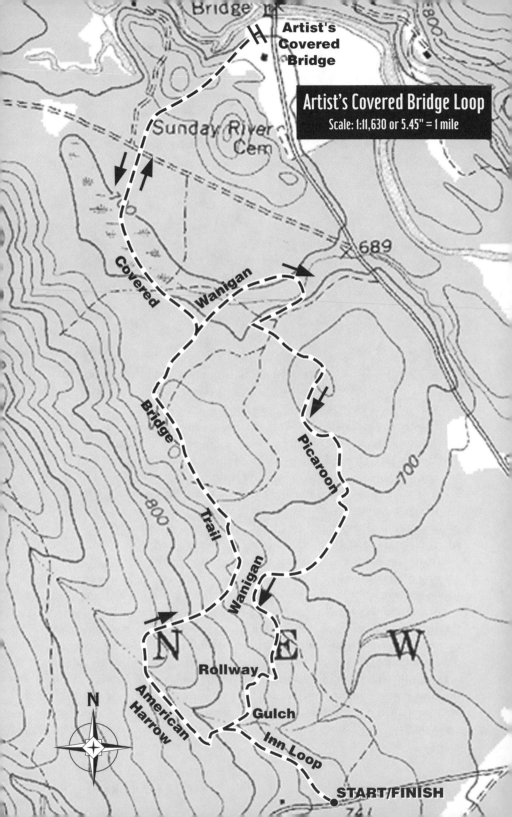

along a brook. Better snowshoers can try the 2.0-mile burst up to the Locke Mountain summit (1,250 elevation gain). They will be rewarded with valley views at the top, but the last pitch is challenging.

Intermediate and advanced skiers will find trails for their abilities in the upper half of the network, where routes like David's Drop and Bruce's Bust will get the heart rate up. Beginner skiers will find gentle and winding trails in the lower portion of the trail network; frequent maps and signs are posted as navigational tools. Many of the trails take their names from a couple of industries that are important to Maine—farming and logging. Cant Dog is named for a hooked metal staff used by loggers. American Harrow takes the name of a plowlike device drawn by horses or tractors.

Throughout the network, skiers have views of the slopes of

Narrow ski trails are part of the Maine woods experience.

Sunday River. On this loop, Barker Mountain is dominant. The 1,400-foot summit was the site of the resort's first chairlift.

The covered bridge is the most popular stop at the cross-country ski center. It is possible to enjoy a simple out-and-back 4.0-mile route to the bridge. Throw in a pitch through a narrow gulch and the playful dips on the Picaroon Trail, and you've got a fun loop with terrain that fluctuates from desert flat to hilly. Also keep your eyes out for a few manmade attractions along the way: benches, totem poles, swinging chairs, and ski-pole wind chimes.

There are a couple of intersections at which the route crosses trails used by snowmobilers and one road crossing where skiers should take their skis off before continuing.

The loop encompasses several of the trails, like the Inn Loop, American Harrow, Covered Bridge Trail, Picaroon, Wanigan, Rollway, and Gulch. The wide trail begins just outside the center, enters the woods, and passes a snow stake that details Mother Nature's contribution to winter. Just follow the signs pointing to the covered bridge and pass through the trail junctions. Initially flat, the trail gets hilly gradually once it connects to American Harrow and offers a few short, zippy downhills along the way. American Harrow leads to the Covered Bridge Trail, which briefly opens up to views of Barker Mountain before returning to the cover of the forest. At the 1.75-mile mark, the Covered Bridge Trail crosses a road (about 0.25 mile from the bridge). Once you are on the other side, ski to a clearing by a white home with a green roof. The bridge will soon be in sight.

Take a rest at the bridge or munch on a snack before returning along the same route. This time, take winding Wanigan from the Covered Bridge Trail to Picaroon, a rolling ride through a white pine forest. Picaroon enters a clearing, where if you are skiing in the morning on a sunny day, the sun will warm your face. The trail reenters the woods before hooking up with Wanigan for a few up-and-down pitches. Rollway is short and sweet: It leads to the gentle ascent up Gulch, a narrow notch in the woods. The terrain will soon look familiar as the loop rejoins the Inn Loop and leads back to the warmth of the ski center.

Directions at a glance

0.0 Leave the cross-country center heading northwest via the Inn Loop Trail.

0.3 Bear left for 100 feet before turning right on American Harrow, where trail gets hilly.

1.0 Turn left on Covered Bridge Trail.

1.75 Take off skis to cross road.

2.0 Reach covered bridge. Return via same route.

2.25 Cross road, again.

2.5 Bear right onto Wanigan.

2.8 Turn left on Picaroon, taking you through white pine forest.

3.6 Turn left onto Wanigan.

3.9 Turn right on Rollway and follow it 100 feet.

3.9 Turn left on Gulch.

4.2 Turn left on Inn Loop and follow it 0.3 mile back to the ski center.

How to get there

From Bethel, travel on Route 26 east for 2.2 miles. Turn left on Sunday River Road, then follow it 2.2 miles to the inn and cross-country ski center on the right.

Mount Blue State Park's Maple Trail
Mount Blue State Park, Weld, Maine

Type of trail: ▬▬▬

Distance: 10 miles round-trip

Terrain: A winding ski through the woods of a Maine State Park

Trail difficulty: Most difficult

Surface quality: Tracked after storms

Time: 4 hours

Food and facilities: Mount Blue State Park in winter has limited facilities. There is no water, but pit toilets are located at the trailhead on Center Hill Road. There is also an ice rink at the parking area. Nearby Weld is a small town with small town stores. The Weld General Store (207–585–2231) not only has sandwiches but also rents snowshoes. The Village Variety (207–585–2508), commonly referred to as "the other store," has pizza and sandwiches. Rumford and Farmington has plenty of places to stay overnight. In Weld, Lake Webb House (207–585–2479) is for those who want to stay nearby. There is a small trail fee to use Mount Blue State Park.

Phone numbers: For information, call Mount Blue State Park at (207) 585–2261.

Mount Blue State Park has that remote feel to it. Though about a two and one half-hour drive from Bangor and less than two hours from Portland, the 5,000-acre park is like a walk on the wild side. From winter headquarters on Center Hill Road, just the panorama of a shimmering Webb Lake below and the frosty Tumbledown Mountain Range (and more) in the distance is worth the drive.

The park, which attracts some 60,000 visitors per year, has 14.0 miles of cross-country ski trails. This is also snowmobile country. Skiers and snowshoers have the option of using the snowmobile trails, too. Snowshoers are asked to stay off the ski trails. But, snowshoe-only trails may be cut in the future. A ranger at Mount Blue suggested that snowshoers head to the Center Hill Picnic Area, a 1.2-mile drive along Center Hill Road from the ski trailhead, and try the 0.5-mile loop there. He also thought it might make a good shoe and slide (bring your own plastic sleds).

It was in the summer of 1798 that the first farm in the area was settled near the wooded shoulders of the Tumbledown Range. Trappers and farmers worked the heavy forests, and by 1870, Weld had swelled to its

peak population of 1,130. In its heyday, the town was home to cheese and canning factories, a tannery, and a shoe factory. Farmers had a rough time during the Great Depression of the 1930s. Soon thereafter, the state swooped in, and in 1935, it created the park after the population of Weld had dwindled below 500. The park has grown since the 1930s and has become the second-largest park in Maine's state system.

Rangers cut the first ski trails in 1987. In general, they are narrow and not at all like the widely groomed skate lanes at touring centers or on logging roads. Some skiers complain, wanting wider lanes, but the ski trails, thin and winding, are just fine the way they are. They do widen from time to time when they are part of old logging roads.

The trails are groomed and tracked after snow falls. For the most part, the system is more intermediate and advanced, but beginners will be able to tackle portions of the network. Skiers will find five trails, ranging from 0.5 mile to

Snow teams up with the mixed forests in Mount Blue State Park to create a tunnel-like effect as a skier glides along.

10.0 miles in length. Each trail is also given a color. Signs are well placed, but distances are not indicated, and there aren't any indicator maps, save the one at the trailhead.

Nonetheless, the trails are easy to follow as they roll through apple orchards, old farmland, softwoods, and hardwoods. The trails are sheltered and don't afford many mountain views. But skiers on the longest loop—the Maple Trail—will have views of Tumbledown, Big Jackson, and Little Jackson. A climb up a spur trail to Hedgehog Hill is where the far-ranging vistas can be found.

The easiest skis are the Moose (green), Fox (orange), and Central (yellow) Trails. The Central Trail leaves the park headquarters and is the main connector trail. It runs through a small apple orchard and past a snow-covered cemetery, before hooking up with the rest of the network.

Directions at a glance

0.0 Leave the trailhead by the sign for "Ski Trails," heading north.

0.3 Cross Center Hill Road and turn right on Maple Trail.

0.7 Stay on Maple Trail; Birch Trail enters right.

2.0 Cross Center Hill Road.

2.3 Turn right on Maple Trail.

5.2 Spur trail leads right to Hedgehog Hill (approximately midway in the tour).

5.9 Turn right on Maple Trail.

7.9 Turn right on Maple Trail.

8.9 Cross Center Hill Road and turn left by sign to parking area.

9.3 Turn left and cross Center Hill Road, which leads back to the parking area.

The 1.0-mile-long Moose Trail loop is a pleasant jaunt through red pine and harvested hardwoods, while the 0.5-mile Fox Trail runs through old farmland. For more of a challenge, take the 2.0-mile-long Birch Trail loop (blue). The trail follows two ridgelines through evergreens and hardwoods.

The premiere trip is the 10.0-mile-long Maple Trail (red). This is where most of the Mount Blue "regulars" ski. The loop can be done in either direction. The trail winds through the woods, follows an old power line, and passes by a couple of old farm houses with mountain vistas, before it winds back into the forest. Because it runs through clear-cut areas, the Maple Trail is laced with hardwood and softwood trees. The trail has a few steep hills to climb. First-timers should leave about four hours to do it. The short spur trail up Hedgehog Hill is a worthy climb.

How to get there

To reach Weld, travel on Route 156 from Wilton or Route 142 from Dixfield. From the junction of Routes 156 and 142 in Weld, follow the signs to Mount Blue State Park. Bear left after 0.5 mile. It is 1.5 miles to park headquarters on Center Hill Road from Weld. The trailhead is on the right side of the road.

The Birches

The Birches Ski Touring Center, Rockwood, Maine

Type of trail: ━━ ◀ ⬤⬤⬤

Distance: 2.8 to 12.0 miles, depending on trail chosen

Terrain: The nearly 3.0-mile beginner loop is gentle and rolling with a thriller of a downhill to wrap things up, while the Poplar Hill Trail is a long day with rewarding lake and mountain vistas.

Trail difficulty: Easiest to more difficult (option)

Surface quality: Skate and track set

Time: 1–4 hours skiing

Food and facilities: The Birches Ski Touring Center is a full-service winter resort. Cross-country skis and snowshoe rentals are available in the ski shop, as are lessons. Moonlight tours and other events like the Mount Kineo Challenge (the third weekend in March) are offered. There is a wax room. The rustic lodge has soothing fireplaces and serves up breakfast, lunch, and dinner. For do-it-yourselfers, there are small grocery stores in Rockwood, like the North Woods Store and Moose River Country Store. The Birches has several overnight accommodations to choose from. There are twenty log cabins, several wilderness yurts, and rooms in the lodge. Snowshoes are allowed on all trails. A system of snowshoe-only trails is planned for the future. You can rent snowmobiles or try ice fishing. Trail pass fee also includes use of sauna, hot tub, and showers.

Phone numbers: The number for the Birches Resort is (800) 825–WILD.

The Birches is off the beaten path, on the edge of Maine's vast wilderness. The 30 miles of groomed trails over the mostly wooded terrain offer the ever-changing forest as a backdrop. Owned by brothers Bill Willard and John Willard, a University of Maine graduate who studied forestry, the resort encompasses 11,000 acres of wildlands on the shores of Moosehead and Brassua Lakes. The rocky monolith called Mount Kineo sits off Moosehead's frozen shore and is quite the sight from a table at the wooded lodge. Throw in miles of local snowmobile trails and the solid lake, and it seems the choices of where to ski or snowshoe are limitless.

A place like The Birches has to have a colorful history, and it does. A logging contractor named Oz Fahey built the lodge in the 1930s. The logging industry took a nosedive as the country foundered in the Great

The Birches
Scale: 1:23,150 or 2.74" = 1 mile

The Birches Center
START/FINISH
Rockwood Trail
Beginner's Loop
Racoon Trail
Maine Trail
Baker Trail
Moose Trail
3 Sisters Trail
GNP Road
Deer Trail
Poplar Hill Trail
Poplar Hill Loop (optional) 3 miles
Poplar Hill Yurt

ROCKWOOD STRIP (TIRINBKP)

N

Depression. But Fahey had a loyal crew. They stayed on to work for room and board. Fahey decided to go into the sporting business, and turned his property into a camp. His house became the lodge, now complete with fireplace, a library, and mounted deer and fish on the walls. Cabins were built beside the main lodge. The Fahey reign lasted until a cosmetic company president bought the lodge in 1960. Then he sold it four years later. For five years, the camp lay dormant, until John Willard's dad bought it. Reopened in 1970, the place is now a four-season spot for all sorts of outdoor recreation. Willard started cutting ski trails in 1974 after scouring area topographical maps. Some trails were old overgrown jeep and logging trails. Most were built from scratch.

It might seem odd for snowshoers and skiers to share a place with snowmobilers. Willard purposefully routed the snowmobile trails out around the perimeter of the ski trails so that the two would only meet at one intersection.

About half the network is skate groomed, while the entire network is tracked for classical skiers. So, we've got two loops here. One is for beginner skiers, the other for those looking for a day-long workout on skate or classic skis.

At just under 3.0 miles, the Rockwood, Raccoon, Moose, Maine Trails Loop is a fun loop, complete with plenty of deer tracks, a chance to scamper up to a yurt, and a thriller of a downhill. Skiers will have to take their skis off twice to cross the Great Northern Paper Company Road.

The Rockwood Trail is a narrow and winding route through the low-lying woods. The animals in the area (snowshoe hares, deer, etc.) are attracted to the streams and wetlands, which accounts for their tracks. The trail runs through softwoods to hardwoods and has a mellow uphill grade before crossing the road and handing off to the Raccoon Trail, a mostly level, winding path. The Moose Trail crosses a frozen wetland area before linking up to the Maine Trail. Just off the Maine Trail (after crossing the GNP road), look for the sign for the Lookout/Overlook Trail. It's a steep climb so beginners might be best to take off the skis, but follow the trail and bear right to the yurt. If you brought your lunch, this is a good spot to eat. Look down through the trees to Moosehead Lake and Mount Kineo. Back on the wide-open Maine Trail, glance through the trees at the lake before getting in that tuck for about a 0.8-mile cruise back to the lodge.

Those skiers looking for a long, challenging ski should try the 12-mile out-and-back optional ski to the Poplar Hill yurt by the shores of Brassua Lake. Parts of the terrain undulate like a rollercoaster. There are a few gradual hills, but the trail also twists and turns, while putting the Jackman Mountain Range bordering Canada on display.

The wide, skater-friendly Maine Trail is the starting point with its mellow uphill to Moose Trail, which has a slight downhill slant. On Moose, pass by a pond created in 1999 and the yurt that overlooks it. Though Moose leads to the Deer Trail, look for moose tracks on Deer, a nice wide-open pathway through low softwoods and brush. The Poplar Hill Trail comes next. Ski through the open field and low-lying trees. At the height of land, gaze up at the immense, open sky, revealing distant mountains. Begin a snakelike descent, winding through the forest and by a bog. After the bog, the trail turns sharply left by an old, unused logging road. Cruise downhill and see Brassua Lake through the trees. Stay to the right on the Poplar Hill Trail because a new trail goes left and leads to the Brassua Lake Dam. Follow the rolling terrain through mixed forests past the Poplar Hill Loop, eventually coming to the yurt overlooking the lake at the top of a knoll. Lunch in the yurt or at the outdoor picnic tables, or follow the path to the lake shore. Check out the nearby island on the lake.

The ski back is equally rewarding, a gradual descent virtually all the way to the lodge. Return via the Poplar Hill Trail. If you are feeling particularly fit, add 3.0 miles to the trip by skiing the Poplar Hill Loop Trail near the yurt. Back on the Poplar Hill Trail, stay on it, then bear right off the road again. Climb back to the height of land and then enjoy the downhill after expending a little effort. Cruise down to the Deer Trail to the left. On occasion glance back at the mountains. The 3 Sisters Trail is next, a narrower and curvy downhill swath that leads to the thickening woods of the Baker Trail. Fly down over the bridge and just dip back uphill. Then find the Maine Trail and cruise back.

A skier takes a breather by a yurt at The Birches in Rockwood. The yurt, a Mongolian style tent, can be used as a warming hut or overnight shelter.

How to get there

From Greenville, turn left at the light on Routes 6/15 and travel 21.6 miles to Rockwood. Turn right by the sign for the Birches after the Moose River Country Store. Follow the signs and go over the bridge. Then turn right. At 0.9 mile, bear right again and go another 1.1 miles to The Birches.

Mount Kineo

The Birches Ski Touring Center, Rockwood, Maine

Type of trail: (symbols)

Also used by: Hikers, snowmobilers

Distance: 7.2 miles round-trip

Terrain: From the flat tundralike quality of Moosehead Lake to the short steep pitches of Mount Kineo, this is a well-diversified snowshoe/ski adventure. Not for the meek.

Trail difficulty: More difficult

Surface quality: Snowmobile packed

Time: 4–5 hours

Food and facilities: The Birches Ski Touring Center has cross-country ski and snowshoe rentals in the ski shop. The lodge serves up breakfast, lunch, and dinner. There are small grocery stores in Rockwood, like the North Woods Store and Moose River Country Store. The Birches has several overnight accommodations to choose from. There are twenty log cabins, several wilderness yurts, and rooms in the lodge. At Kineo Cove, The Kineo House is open in winter, serving lunch and drinks. No bathrooms or water available on the trail.

Phone numbers: Call the Birches Resort at (800) 825–WILD. The Moosehead Lake Region Chamber of Commerce is (207) 695–3440. The Maine Bureau of Parks and Recreation can be reached at (207) 289–3824 out of state, and (800) 332–1501 within Maine.

Mount Kineo could be the most distinctive landmark on the largest lake in the Northeast—Moosehead Lake. From the wooded summit of the nearly 1,800-foot peak, one can climb an observation tower and see the kingdom of Moosehead and beyond. The panorama from the deck above the pines is striking. There are miles of coves and inlets below. The frozen lake is more like a vast tundra. The lake can be abuzz with activity in one direction, while nary a soul can be seen in another. Mountains and trees dominate the landscape. The snow forms a checkerboard pattern on the lake. The hum of snowmobiles can be heard amidst the quiet.

Mount Kineo is a monolith that rises some 800 feet above the lake. The mountain is on a peninsula that begins on the eastern shore and comes within a mile or so of the western shore.

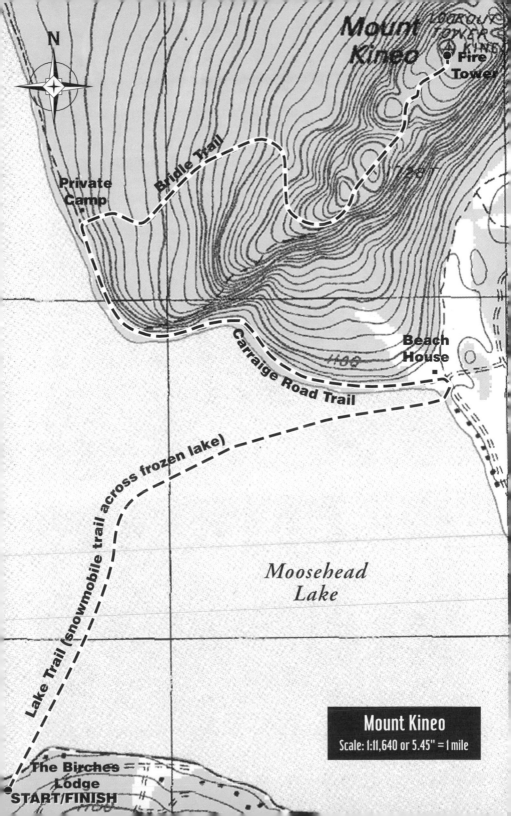

N

Mount
Kineo

LOOKOUT
TOWER
KINEO
Fire
Tower

Private
Camp

Bridle Trail

Carraige Road Trail

Beach
House

Lake Trail (snowmobile trail across frozen lake)

Moosehead
Lake

The Birches
Lodge
START/FINISH

Mount Kineo
Scale: 1:11,640 or 5.45" = 1 mile

In the nonsnow months, the trails of Mount Kineo are popular with hikers. They can take a shuttle boat from The Birches or Rockwood Landing, hire a boat or take their own. In winter, unless one wants to use a snowmobile, access is on foot.

Mount Kineo's 700-foot-high cliffs are home to rare plants and peregrine falcons. During his 1857 trip to Maine, Henry David Thoreau climbed the mountain. From after the Civil War until the 1930s, the Mount Kineo House Hotel called the land home and was the largest lake hotel in America. On top of the mountain, the Maine Forest Service once maintained a fire tower. Now there is the observation deck.

There are a few snowmobile trails that lead from Rockwood to Kineo. They are marked on the ice with wooden posts. The Lake Trail, which runs 2.0 miles from the Birches Resort to Kineo, is but one option. Check with locals for others. Be sure to also check about the conditions on the lake before venturing out onto it. Also, stick to the marked trails. Though you'll be sharing them with snowmobiles, those are the most-traveled routes. Howling winds can make travel unpleasant. Snow conditions vary on the lake. When the winter brings much snow, locals talk about using their skate skis on the snowmobile trails to ski to the mountain. But when winter isn't as generous, snowshoes or ice skates can be used on the icy surface to Kineo.

This is a view of frozen Moosehead Lake as seen from atop the Mount Kineo platform.

Skiing up the Kineo trails probably isn't a good idea. If you are skiing to the mountain, count on bringing your snowshoes for the trek to the tower and then using the skis to get back to Rockwood.

The flat and frozen Lake Trail leaves from the front of The Birches Lodge. It is well marked with arrows and wooden posts. The trail passes a few cabins before venturing out onto the ice. Be cognizant that you are on a snowmobile trail. Kineo stands before you. The trail goes across the lake and swings to the right as it approaches the towering cliffs. Ice fishermen might be trying their luck. After about 2.0 miles, you reach shore. Turn left by the yellow boathouse, and you will soon reach the trailhead.

The Carriage Road follows the shore's edge and winds under the dramatic cliffs. The Carriage Road passes a junction with Indian Trail. The trail is fairly rocky and isn't the best in winter. Continue another 0.2 mile to the junction with the Bridle Trail, then turn right. Start a moderate climb through the mixed forest and pass a private camp. The trail snakes up the mountain, steeply in places. At an unsigned junction, bear left up the steep but short incline. However, both options lead to the same place.

About 0.4 mile from the summit, the Bridle Trail and Indian Trail come together. Take some time to admire the views of the Kineo Cottages and the shores of Rockwood. The blue-blazed Bridle Trail now heads to the summit. It will dip down before rising again quickly. Then, behold the tower. Climb and enjoy.

Return along the same route. Once again, stop to admire the views by the outcrop near the Indian Trail and bear to the right on the Bridle Trail. Follow it back down past the brown home and turn left on the Carriage Road, which leads back to the trailhead. If you have the energy, visit the Kineo House for lunch before taking the Lake Trail back across Moosehead to The Birches.

Directions at a glance

0.0 Leave using the Lake Trail (a snowmobile trail) directly outside the Birches Lodge, going north, then northeast.

2.0 Reach the Kineo Peninsula and turn left by yellow beach house. The trailhead is just beyond that. Follow the Carriage Road.

2.5 Turn right on the Bridle Trail, soon passing a private camp, starting a moderate climb.

3.2 Reach junction with Indian Trail. Stay left and continue 0.4 mile to summit.

3.6 Reach summit and fire tower. Return via Bridle Trail.

4.0 Reach junction with Indian Trail and bear right on Bridle Trail.

4.7 Turn left on Carriage Road.

5.2 Turn right back on Lake Trail; take it 2.0 miles across lake back to land.

How to get there

From Greenville, turn left at the light on Routes 6/15 and travel 21.6 miles to Rockwood, then turn right by the sign for The Birches after the Moose River Country Store. Follow the signs and go over the bridge. Then turn right. After 0.9 mile, bear right again and go another 1.1 miles to The Birches.

Gulf Hagas

Little Lyford Pond Camps and Lodge, Greenville, Maine

Type of trail:	▬▬▬ 🌀
Also used by:	Hikers, small portion by snowmobilers
Distance:	12.0 miles one-way to Little Lyford Pond Camps and Lodge; 8.2 miles round-trip from lodge to Gulf Hagas and back; 12.0 miles one-way from lodge back to Greenville.
Terrain:	Gulf Hagas is the "Grand Canyon of Maine" with dramatic drops and views.
Trail difficulty:	More difficult
Surface quality:	Ungroomed
Time:	3 full days for entire journey; 4–5 hours for 8.2 mile round-trip only
Food and facilities:	Little Lyford Pond Camps and Lodge (LLPC) is a homey sports camp with nine cabins. Overnighters get three meals a day with a vegetarian flavor, though poultry and fish are served as well. Electricity? Forget about it. Showers? How about a sauna. Running water? Not exactly, but it's provided. Each cabin has its own outhouse round back. The camp keeps in touch with the outside world via radio and for emergencies, a cellular phone.

For those who don't want to ski in, arrangements can be made via LLPC for snowmobile and sled-dog rides or flights in. LLPC will also take your gear in for you for a fee. LLPC does not have snowshoe or cross-country ski rentals, though chances are they'll have a pole or maybe even a ski for you should something happen to yours. For rentals, try North Woods Outfitters in Greenville (207–695–3288). No trail fee. |
| **Phone numbers:** | Little Lyford Pond Camps and Lodge can be reached by calling (207) 280–0016. |

The deep and narrow slate cliffs of Gulf Hagas are dramatic in winter. Ice forms on the walls, creating avenues of vertical blue. Snow covers the pine forest at the top of the canyon, and the walls eventually narrow to create falls, polls, and chutes. No wonder Gulf Hagas is called the "Grand Canyon of Maine."

The craggy gulf is along the West Branch of the Pleasant River. During a 4.0-mile run, the river drops 400 feet. Just off the Appalachian Trail, Gulf Hagas was once a spot for logging. Huge trees would be transported down the river, though one might wonder how the timber was fed

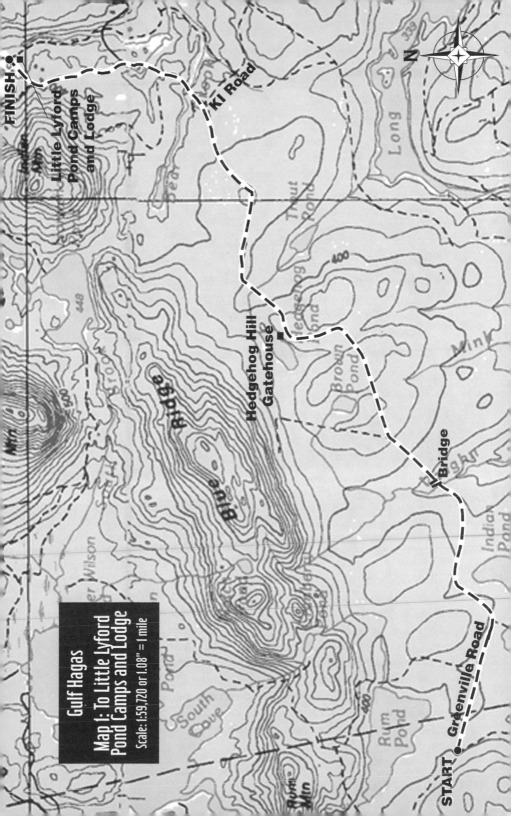

FINISH

Little Lyford Pond Camps and Lodge

Indian Mtn

Mtn

KI Road

Long A

339

N

Sear Brook

Trout Pond

400

Hedgehog Pond

Hedgehog Hill Gatehouse

Blue Ridge

Brown Pond

Mink

448

400

West Branch Pleasant River

Carl A. Wilson

Bridge

Pond To

Indian Pond

South Cove

Rum Pond

400

Rum Mtn

Gulf Hagas

Map 1: To Little Lyford Pond Camps and Lodge

Scale: 1:59,720 or 1.08" = 1 mile

START Greenville Road

Directions at a glance

To Little Lyford Pond Camps and Lodge

0.0   Leave Rum Ridge area on Greenville Road, a logging road, heading east.

5.0   Cross bridge.

7.5   Pass Hedgehog Hill Gatehouse.

10.0   Reach a junction and turn left on Katahdin Iron Works (KI) Road.

11.0   Bear left on logging road by LLPC sign.

12.25 Turn right at LLPC and ski down to cabins.

To Gulf Hagas

0.0   Leave lodge via trail to Gulf Hagas, heading southeast.

1.0   Turn left onto snowmobile trail and cross bridge. In 100 yards, turn right on trail marked by surveyor's tape. After a few feet, look for sign for Little Lyford on left.

2.5   Turn right at sign for Gulf Hagas Rim Trail.

2.7   Reach Head of the Gulf spur.

3.0   Reach Billings Falls.

3.7   Reach Buttermilk Falls.

4.1   Reach The Jaws and return via the same route.

5.7   Turn left at Gulf Hagas Rim Trail sign.

7.2   Turn left on snowmobile trail and cross bridge. In 100 yards, turn right at sign for Little Lyford; follow it 1.0 mile back to the lodge.

through where the cannon narrows. The last big logging took place in the 1930s. Now, the gulf is a Registered National Landmark.

The gulf is located between White Cap Mountain and the Barren-Chairback Range. In winter, getting there can be quite the trip. Plan a weekend. If you decide to ski to the lodge rather than take a snowmobile, dog sled, or flight in, plan on a 12-mile ski one day, then overnighting at Little Lyford Pond Camps and Lodge, and about an 8.0-mile ski/snowshoe trip the next day. Ski back 12.0 miles the third day.

Little Lyford Pond Camps and Lodge, run by Bob LeRoy and Arlene Hadley-LeRoy, is an old logging camp turned sporting camp that was built in the late 1800s. It's a bit like the Land That Time Forgot, with no electricity and its cabin roofs covered with snow. Located in the Pleasant

High granite walls, tall pines, and dramatic drops are part of the Gulf Hagas experience.

River Valley along the West Branch of the Pleasant River, the camp is surrounded by mountains, like Elephant, Indian, White Cap, and Baker. About 30 miles of cross-country ski trails have been cut, providing access to 400,000 acres of paper company-owned land. Don't expect a grooming machine out this way. To groom the trails, the LeRoys might go out with snowshoes to pack the snow down. Signs are at a minimum, but well placed. Follow the blue squares out and the blue diamonds in. That's the signage on the trails with the occasional blue LLPC thrown in for good measure.

Little Lyford is the jumping off place for a winter Gulf Hagas trip.

But first you've got to get there.

Access to the camp is along an unplowed, multiple-use logging road. The longest ski into the camp, along flat to rolling terrain with views out to Maine's central mountains, can be just over 12 miles. But sometimes the logging company plows the road a bit, and the ski in can narrow down to 9 miles. Nevertheless, it's a good four hours in to the camp along the Greenville Road. Carrying gear isn't necessary. Bob can haul it in behind a snowmobile. Most people ski in. Snowmobile, dog sled, and plane are other options.

The ski along the Greenville Road is fairly easy, but it's the distance and anticipation that makes it more difficult. Snowmobiles use the road too. It's basically 10.0 miles from the start to a junction with the Katahdin

Iron Works Road and then about 2.5 miles from there. Mountain ranges are off in the distance with peaks like Elephant Mountain, the site of a B-52 crash, and White Cap Mountain, where the Appalachian Trail wanders.

When descending into the camps, don't be surprised if a barking dog or two greet you. The woodstove will be going in the cabin. Hot water for hot chocolate or spiced cider will be simmering, and huge, chocolate chip cookies will be ready for munching.

After a much-needed sauna, rest up for the next day.

On the following day, ski or snowshoe from the lodge to Gulf Hagas, but once there, either use snowshoes or winter hiking boots. Forget about skiing. The Rim Trail is unforgiving.

The 8.0-mile round-trip ski/snowshoe begins outside the lodge and heads into the narrowness of the woods. The first 1.0 mile winds through the pine. It's about 0.5 mile to the first look at the West Branch of the Pleasant River, before you dip back into the dense forest and encounter a quick, steep pitch back up to the banks of the rolling river. Up ahead, the route opens up to a bridge and logging road used by snowmobilers. Cross the bridge by making a left, and then ski about 100 yards before turning right into the woods. A few feet into the trail, look for the LLPC sign on the left. Dip down and meander through the tunnellike trees. At about 2.0 miles, a sign alerts you to the Appalachian Trail. In about 0.5 mile, you'll come to a signpost and turn right on the Gulf Hagas Rim Trail. Ski down about 0.2 mile to the Head of the Gulf, giving you that first glimpse of the canyon. Leave your skis. Switch to snowshoes. Follow the Rim Trail as it goes up and down along the edge of the canyon. The various spur trails are well worth taking in for the vistas. The views get better as the trail continues. The best views? The vista down from Billings Falls is at the top of the list. Many people stop here, have lunch, and head back. Better, continue on to Buttermilk Falls, where the canyon narrows dramatically. At The Jaws, the canyon squeezes in even tighter. Return via the Rim Trail and the ski trail back to LLPC.

How to get there

From Greenville, go past the blinking light on Main Street and turn right on Pleasant Street. Follow it some 4 miles, until the plowing stops at a sign that says RUM RIDGE. Or arrange to meet with a staff member of Little Lyford Pond Camps at the North Woods Outfitters, Main Street, Greenville, to lead you to the trailhead.

Big Lyford Pond

Little Lyford Pond Camps and Lodge, Greenville, Maine

Type of trail: ▬▬◣ ⬤

Distance: 12.0 miles round-trip from Little Lyford Pond Camps and Lodge to Big Lyford Pond and back.

Terrain: Ski through narrow, tunnel-like trail near a couple of ponds with native trout.

Trail difficulty: Easiest to more difficult

Surface quality: Ungroomed, but skier tracked

Time: 4 hours

Food and facilities: Little Lyford Pond Camps and Lodge is a homey sports camp with nine cabins. Overnighters get three meals a day with a vegetarian flavor, though fish and poultry are served as well. Electricity? Forget about it. Showers? How about a sauna. Running water? Not exactly, but it's provided. Each cabin has its own outhouse round back. The camp keeps in touch with the outside world via radio and for emergencies, a cellular phone.

For those who don't want to ski in, arrangements can be made via LLPC for snowmobile and sled-dog rides or flights in. LLPC will also take your gear in for you for a fee. LLPC does not have snowshoe or cross-country ski rentals, though chances are they'll have a pole or maybe even a ski for you should something happen to yours. For rentals, try North Woods Outfitters in Greenville (207–695–3288). No trail fee.

Phone numbers: Little Lyford Pond Camps and Lodge can be reached by calling (207) 280–0016.

Native brook trout live in the two ponds at Little Lyford Pond Camps and Lodge. Maybe along the trails you'll spot the tracks of moose, deer, or fisher cats. At night, off in the distance, perhaps hear the howl of a coyote.

Little Lyford Pond Camps and Lodge is the spot used as base camp before heading into Gulf Hagas. Though the "Grand Canyon of Maine" is a must-see, it isn't the only journey worth making from the camps.

Going to Big Lyford Pond and a junction about 0.5 mile beyond it is a rewarding trip, taking you through marshlike areas with views of the scars on Baker Mountain and along the banks of the West Branch of the Pleasant River.

Big Lyford Pond

Bridge

N

Baker Mountain Brook Crossing

Little Lyford Ponds

Little Lyford Pond Camps and Lodge

START/FINISH

Big Lyford Pond
Scale: 1:45,530 or 1.49" = 1 mile

Loop trails encircle both of the Little Lyford Ponds. Leave the lodge on the trail to the ponds that leads across the open area by the lodge before ducking into the shelter of the forest. In about 100 yards, the trail for the first pond breaks left. The views of Indian and Baker Mountains are quite beautiful here, well worth a look. Just beyond the first trail, another path leads to the second pond, a bit more secluded than the first.

After passing the ponds, the trail begins the first of three crossings into boggy areas. Be forewarned, the trails dip near the water, and unsuspecting skiers might have to put on the brakes rather quickly. It makes for interesting crossings in soothing surroundings.

Near the 2.0-mile mark, the trail shoots through a clearing, allowing you to view slides on the side of Baker Mountain. This is a good spot to look for moose tracks. Off by the riverside, a short spur trail leads to the river banks. Follow it, turn around, and enjoy that view. The trail narrows at this point and meanders through young new pines. Near the 3.0-mile mark, cross Baker Mountain Brook and continue through the woods. Just before the 4.0-mile mark, look for an obvious left into a clearing. Take it. From that amphitheater, you have striking views of the mountains. After taking in the show, return to the trail, which takes an obvious right at the 5.0-mile mark by a sign saying SKI TRAIL. The ski trail reaches Big Lyford Pond over a bridge. Actually, to see the pond itself involves some bushwhacking. It's best to either stop here or continue onward and upward for about 0.5 mile to a junction with a snowmobile trail, also a decent lunch spot and a place to take in the panoramas. Return via the same way, rolling down the hill, crossing the bridge, and

Directions at a glance

0.0   Leave the lodge via the trail to Little Lyford Ponds, going north. At 100 yards, trail to first pond leaves left.

0.25 Trail to second pond leaves left.

2.0   Enter clearing. View Baker Mountain to left. Short spur trail to West Branch of Pleasant River is on right.

3.0   Cross Baker Mountain Brook.

3.7   Option exists to turn left into clearing with striking mountain vistas.

5.0   Bear right at sign saying SKI TRAIL.

5.5   Cross bridge to Big Lyford Pond.

6.0   Continue to intersection with snowmobile road, return via same route.

6.5   Recross bridge.

7.0   Bear left by sign saying SKI TRAIL.

9.0   Cross Baker Mountain Brook.

12.0 Reach lodge.

It's a 12-mile ski from Greenville to the remote Little Lyford cabins. From there, skiers and snowshoers have a base of operation to explore the Maine wilderness.

ending up back at the lodge. On the way back, if you haven't done so already, visit the two Little Lyford Ponds.

How to get there

From Greenville, go past the blinking light on Main Street and turn right on Pleasant Street. Follow it some 4.0 miles, until the plowing stops at a sign that says RUM RIDGE. Or arrange to meet with a staff member of Little Lyford Pond Camps at the North Woods Outfitters, Main Street, Greenville, to lead you to the trailhead.

Lily Bay State Park

Lily Bay State Park, Beaver Cove, Maine

Type of trail:	▭▭▭ ◉
Also used by:	Snowmobilers (portions)
Distance:	4.6-mile loop
Terrain:	The winding trails through a state park serve up vistas of a frozen Moosehead Lake.
Trail difficulty:	Easiest to more difficult
Surface quality:	Skier tracked, snowmobile packed
Time:	2 hours (skiing), 4½ hours (shoeing)
Food and facilities:	Greenville, 9 miles away, is the place for supplies and lodging. Grocery stores can be found at both Indian Hill Plaza and Moosehead Center. Cross-country ski and snowshoe rentals can be had from Northwoods Outfitters (207–695–3288) on Main Street. Kelly's Landing, on Route 6/15 in Greenville Junction, is a restaurant on the lake. So is the Boomchain, closer to town. The local chamber of commerce can help with area accommodations. The Greenwood Motel in Greenville Junction is reasonably priced (800–477–4386). Ice skaters may want to bring their skates for the lake. Pit toilets are available throughout the trek. Bring your own paper just to be safe. Hand-pumped water is available too, but it's best to bring your own.
Phone numbers:	The number for the Moosehead Lake Region Chamber of Commerce is (207) 695–3440. The Maine Bureau of Parks and Recreation is at (207) 287–3824 (out of state) and (800) 332–1501 (within Maine).

The largest lake in New England sits in the north of Maine. Greenville, a small town buzzing with snowmachines and sea planes, is the gateway to Moosehead Lake, a glacier-made basin that covers 117 square miles. The 40-mile-long, deep and chilly lake harbors landlocked salmon, trout, and togue. Ice shanties on the lake are evidence of man's attempt to fish for the scaly creatures even in the deep chill of winter.

The Moosehead Lake region is wild. Already some 1,000 feet above sea level, the flat-topped Mount Kineo rises 800 feet more from a peninsula on the lake. Bear, deer, and moose are common visitors to the area. No doubt these animals proved useful to the early settlers of the area, who over 10,000 years ago hunted, fished, and used flint for tools. The lake was a major hub back then, a port connecting the various river systems.

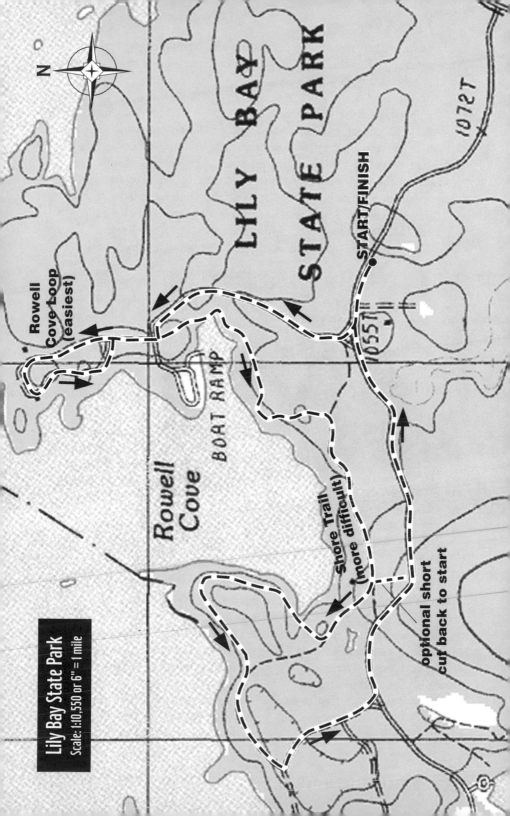

Lily Bay State Park
Scale: 1:10,550 or 6" = 1 mile

N

LILY BAY STATE PARK

START/FINISH

Rowell Cove Loop
(easiest)

Rowell Cove

BOAT RAMP

Shore Trail
(more difficult)

optional short
cut back to start

1072 T

1055 T

The logging trucks are the results the area's being opened to logging and farming back in the 1820s. A generation later, visitors began to come to enjoy the outdoors.

And they still do.

Some 9 miles from Greenville are the 925 acres of Lily Bay State Park. Located on the eastern shore of Moosehead Lake, the park maintains about 8 miles of trails for cross-country skiing and snowshoeing. Lily Bay State Park serves up trails that hug the lake's meandering coastline. Trails also follow the park roads into camping areas, where skiers and snowshoers can gaze at the distant mountains while having lunch.

Be forewarned, the park also has a network of snowmobile trails. The park road is a lane used by both humans and machines. However, there is civilized management of this usage. The wide road allows for skiers on one side and snowmobiles on the other. There are a number of signs indicating this. The 1.4-mile trail that runs from the park entrance to the shore of Moosehead Lake is shared by all users. There are two loop trails—Rowell Cove and Dunn Point—that head through camping areas. These are supposed to be for just skiers but snowmobile tracks indicate otherwise.

The twisted remains of a fallen tree add to the winter scenery on the frozen shores of Moosehead Lake at Lily Bay State Park near Greenville.

Skiers and snowshoers looking for more solitude should best stick to the trail closest to shore, which links the two loops.

The trails begin just beyond the check-in station. Along the way, there are well-stationed maps. Blue signs (with little skiers) show where skiers and snowshoers can go. The trail between Rowell Cove and Dunn Point is blazed in white.

Follow the main trail to Moosehead Lake about 0.2 mile before the Rowell Cove Loop leaves to the right by an island of trees. The loop is 1.4 miles in length and rolls to a gate where skiers bear to the right. The loop now runs through the campground. Just stick to the main road and all will be well. Pass the toilets and hand pumps. Find campsite 17 and turn right for a nice view out to the lake. Explore the lake. Or find site 35 and have a picnic lunch there. The beauty of the park is that the trails lead to spots that allow you to make your own little paths. The Rowell Cove Loop is good for beginners and kids. For those curious about what is behind the loop, the main road leads to a boat launch ramp.

To bring the experience up a notch, take the shore trail, which leaves at the gate junction. The trail meanders along the water's edge, weaving close and far from the shoreline. Better skiers and snowshoers will like this narrow and winding trail. Pine forests and birches dominate the landscape. After about 0.5 mile or so a spur trail branches right to the lakeshore for a good view. Stay straight and the wooded trail will soon come out to another sort of loop, where you'll spot a residence on the right. (*Note:* Those wanting to shorten the loop can turn left and then left again on the main road.) Turn right by the wooden post and head for the other wooden post. The trail is blazed in white and sweeps down through the mixed forest before rising. It's a rollercoaster ride. Birches dominate. Look off through the trees to the shore. The trail takes a hard left and winds up and down before coming back out by a campground road and site 235. Either way will bring you back to the main trail. This is the Dunn Point campground. There is a 0.8-mile loop through it. The shortest way is to turn left and head back to the main trail. Then take a right and be on the wide thoroughfare again. Head up the hill, then enjoy the cruise back to the entrance.

Directions at a glance

0.0 Leave the ranger station on the Park Road, going west.

0.2 Bear right to Rowell Cove Loop.

0.7 Either continue with loop (easy), or turn left at trail sign and pick up more difficult shore trail. Follow winding trail past residence and continue on as it hugs shore.

1.7 Turn left for Dunn Point.

2.5 Turn left on Park Road and return to ranger station.

How to get there

From Greenville, head north from the traffic light in town on the road to Kokadjo. There is a sign for Lily Bay State Park. Travel 9 miles and turn left. The parking area is a short way in.

Fields Pond Nature Center Loop
Holden, Maine

Type of trail:	●●● , ▬▬▬ (portions)
Distance:	About 1.0-mile loop
Terrain:	Flat through the fields with a jaunt along the tall pines, pond vistas.
Trail difficulty:	Easiest
Surface quality:	Ungroomed
Time:	1 hour
Food and facilities:	The Fields Pond Nature Center is open in winter Thursday through Saturday from 10:00 A.M. to 4:00 P.M. and Sunday from 1:00 to 4:00 P.M. The center has rest rooms and water, plus a small gift shop. Snowshoe rentals and trail maps are available. The center has bimonthly animal tracking programs throughout the winter. There is no fee for trail use, but donations are accepted. Afterward, there are numerous restaurants in Brewer, like the Weathervane on Route 1A. Accommodations are plentiful in nearby Bangor. The Super 8 Motel (207–945–5681) is located off I–95 via exit 45B.
Phone numbers:	The Fields Pond Nature Center is at (207) 989–2591. You can reach the Bangor Region Chamber of Commerce at (207) 947–0307.

Tracks are an integral part of snowshoeing and cross-country skiing. People make their own tracks. Just look ahead or behind.

But humans aren't the only ones out in the woods and fields during winter. There are the animals of winter. How often have you snowshoed out in the forest only to see a set of tracks cross the trail and head into the woods? Was it a moose? Maybe it was a deer.

One place to get a handle on which animal makes which tracks is the Maine Audubon Society's Fields Pond Nature Center in Holden. The center opened its doors in 1997 and prides itself on its winter tracking programs, according to the center's director Judy Kellogg Markowsky. On the 170 acres of pine and cedar trees, flat fields, and birdhouses near the shore of Fields Pond, visitors can find the tracks of a number of nature's creatures, like the ruffed grouse, white-tail deer, red fox, red squirrel, deer mouse, masked shrew, and meadow vole. Each of the animals leaves a distinctive pattern in the snow. Though you might not see a deer, you may see the tracks left behind.

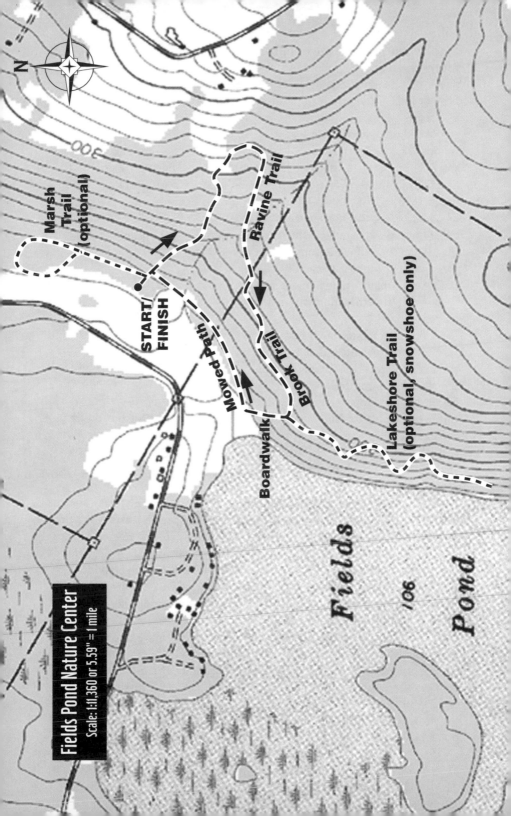

N

Marsh
Trail
(optional)

300

START/
FINISH

Ravine Trail

Mowed Path

Brook Trail

Boardwalk

Lakeshore Trail
(optional, snowshoe only)

Fields Pond

Fields Pond Nature Center
Scale: 1:11,360 or 5.59" = 1 mile

The center is located east of Bangor in the hills above the Penobscot River. There are only about 2.5 miles of trails on the property, but the paths do link up with area snowmobile routes and a hiking trail to Brewer Lake. Still, you have to start somewhere, and the nature center, like many Maine Audubon properties, is suitable for families, children, senior citizens, and those just looking for a winter stroll through the woods. The trails, mostly a series of loops, are good for the beginning snowshoer. Skiers might not find it terribly challenging to ski the flat Marsh Trail and mowed path to the pond (about 0.5 mile total), but it can be done.

A brook passes through the center of the property, and it is the heart of a nearly 1.0-mile-long loop through the property. Generally, the trails don't have many signs, but those utilized in this short circuit are blazed in blue.

A red sign-in station is just outside the nature center; that's where the tour begins. The Ravine Trail is directly ahead and follows the flats for just a bit before leading upward through the pine forest to the top of a ravine. Look down on the brook, still flowing in winter. The trail snakes through the woods and goes across the stream again. Though you might not know it because of the snow, there are stone steps under a couple of spots on the trail. At times, the evergreens are mixed with birches, which give the forest an airy feel. The Ravine Trail ends where the Brook Trail begins as the path heads downward where it runs along the rushing water. Soon enough, a long cedar boardwalk covered in snow will appear. Then, through the leafless trees, you'll see the frozen pond. At the junction, one can take a 0.5-mile snowshoe along the Lakeshore Trail by turning left. The trail, a hilly path, follows the pond shore, crossing over two hills, while offering a few vistas (including one spot with stone benches). The trail goes to the property boundary, marked by orange blazes. It's about 0.5 mile out and back to the boardwalk. To head back to the nature center follow the Brook Trail by crossing over the boardwalk. The trail leads to a field, where by taking a left, you'll head toward a boat launch. Instead take a right, first admiring the white farmhouse, and return to the nature center through the flat fields.

Directions at a glance

0.0 Begin by the red sign-in station. Take the trail directly in front, the Ravine Trail, heading south.

0.3 Go right on the Brook Trail.

0.6 Go straight over the boardwalk, or turn left on the Lakeshore Trail to Brewer Lake.

0.7 After crossing broadwalk turn right to return to the nature center across mowed path.

How to get there

From Brewer and Route 1A, turn onto Gree Point Road. Travel approximately 1.0 mile to a T junction. Turn left on Wiswell Road, continuing for about 1.5 miles. Turn right on Fields Pond Road. The nature center is nearly 1.0 mile down the road on the left.

Baxter State Park Loop

Baxter State Park, Millinocket, Maine

Type of trail:	▰▰▰ ⊛
Also used by:	Hikers, portion by snowmobilers
Distance:	6.0-mile loop
Terrain:	Nearly unobstructed distant Katahdin views, followed by a rollicking narrow ride through the woods
Trail difficulty:	More difficult
Surface quality:	Ungroomed
Time:	2 hours skiing, 6 hours snowshoeing
Food and facilities:	"If you need it, bring it." That's the Baxter mantra. There's no water on this trek. Millinocket's Central Street has food and last-minute items. At the Abol Bridge, a store is open on weekends in winter. There is a portable toilet nearby. At the Abol Beach Picnic Area, you'll find picnic tables and a pit toilet. Millinocket has a few hotels, but about 10 miles from the park on Black Cat Road is New England Outdoor Center's Twin Pines Camp (800–766–7238), a traditional sporting camp with cabins. Skiers and snowshoers can traipse offshore on Millinocket Lake with A-OK Katahdin views. The River Drivers Restaurant on Old Medway Road in Millinocket is a post-Baxter treat. Rentals? Ask at the chamber of commerce on Central Street.
Phone numbers:	Before any winter trip into Baxter State Park, it's best to check in at the park office on 64 Balsam Drive, Millinocket. (Zip code for mailing for a multi-day use application is 04462.) The phone number is (207) 723–5140. The phone number for the Katahdin Area Chamber of Commerce is (207) 723–4443.

Just shy of a mile high, Mount Katahdin dominates the landscape of the more than 200,000 acres in Baxter State Park. About 175 miles of trails exist within the park, along with forty six peaks

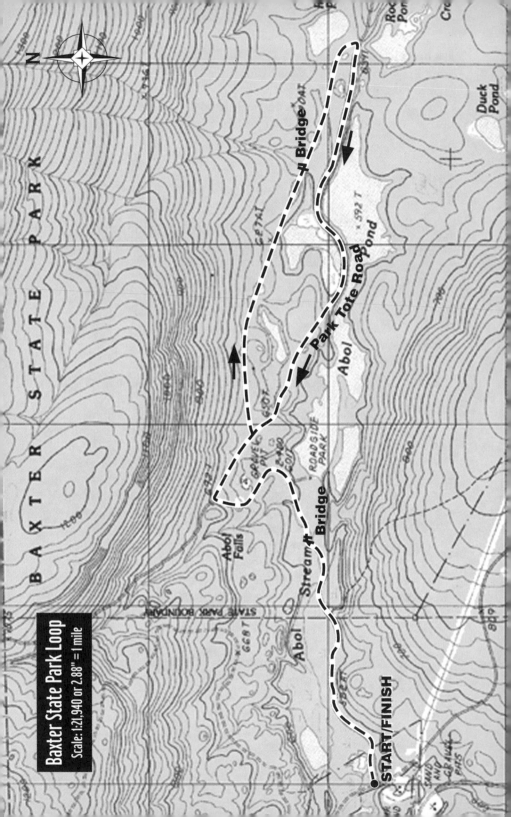

N

Baxter State Park Loop
Scale: 1:21,940 or 2.88" = 1 mile

BAXTER STATE PARK

Duck Pond

Park Tote Road

Bridge

Abol Pond

ROADSIDE PARK

GRAVEL PIT

Abol Falls

STATE PARK BOUNDARY

Abol Stream

Bridge

START/FINISH

Katahdin is the highest mountain in Maine and is a dramatic backdrop for any winter trail adventure.

and ridges. But guess what? It's not all that easy to access the park in winter.

Winter day-users are best off using the southern entrance to the park, about 20 miles from Millinocket. From here, skiers and snowshoers have access to several miles of trails. Though the best views and terrain are farther inside the park, Baxter has some strict winter-use regulations for those who want to venture to the backcountry for skiing and climbing on Maine's highest peak. A minimum of four people in a party are required, and those in the group must have outdoor experience resumes. For an application, contact the park offices at the Millinocket address.

For those who want to sample a sliver of the park, it can be done on the Baxter State Park Loop, a combination of ski trails and the Park Tote Road. The road is open to snowmobiles, with a posted speed limit of twenty miles per hour. Skiers are on that portion for about 1.0 mile. Though the loop is more difficult in nature, it is easiest (and flat) on the section to the Abol Beach Picnic Area. That is a good turnaround point for beginner skiers and snowshoers, an out-and-back trip of just over 3.0 miles.

The loop begins several yards from the Abol Bridge, which spans the West Branch of the Penobscot. Be sure to mosey over to the bridge for the views. Begin the tour from the unmarked parking area, cross Golden Road, and take the road that passes beneath the power lines. It dips down gently to the right, passes through an opened gate, and voilà, there is the sign for the ski trail. Strap on the skis.

A Baxter State Park sign marks the beginning of the ski trail. The sign gives mileage to the Togue Pond Gate via the ski trail and Park Tote Road as 4.0 miles. The trail, which also follows the Appalachian Trail north, is marked with blue cross-country ski signs.

The ski goes past what looks like a gravel pit. A forest fire in 1977 burned this part of the park, and the pit was once a fire break. Because of the fire, you have nearly unobstructed views as new growth trees and posts sprout up through the snow.

The trail bears to the right after about 0.25 mile. Notice the sign indicating 1.5 miles to Abol Pond. Mount Katahdin sits off in the distance to the left. The trail is quite flat. Look for animal tracks, mainly moose, on and off the trail. Abol Stream soon parallels the trail and winds along.

Near the 0.75-mile mark, cross the boundary into the park. There is a boundary sign on a tree. The ski trail veers slightly to the left. Soon thereafter, you encounter a registration box. Visitors should sign in. It's not too far until skiers cross over Abol Stream on a wooden bridge. The trail narrows and is a straight shot through the new growth of trees.

Skiers reach a junction at 1.5 miles. Turn right for the Abol Beach Picnic Area. There are a couple of picnic tables and a toilet available. If the ice is thick enough, ski on the pond. Beginners should turn around here.

The better skiers can save the pond for the trip back.

Directions at a glance

0.0   From parking area turn left by Baxter State Park sign for TOGUE POND GATE via ski trail and Park Tote Road, 4.0 miles.

0.25 Turn right by BSP sign for ABOL POND 1.5 miles, junction with Park Tote Road 1.75 miles, and Togue Pond Gate 4.0 miles.

1.5   Turn right for Abol Beach Picnic Area. Or a quick left and quick right leads to the continuation of the ski trail.

1.75 Cross Park Tote Road. Ski trail continues across the road through woods.

3.0   Turn right on Park Tote Road.

4.0   Turn left on ski trail.

4.25 Quick right and quick left to ski trail.

5.5   Bear left to BSP sign for TOGUE POND GATE via ski trail and Park Tote Road, 4.0 miles. Return to car.

After the junction, there is an island of trees just ahead. The ski trail continues by taking a quick left and quick right. The trail climbs upward and overlooks the pond. It's wiggles up and down until reaching Park Tote Road at 1.75 miles.

The ski trail continues across the road, heads down a gully, and offers up some moderate rollicking hills for the next mile or so. It's quiet, narrow, and sheltered in here. The tunnel effect is peaceful. Look through the trees for huge glacial boulders. At about 2.5 miles, get ready to cross a bridge. It is at the bottom of a nice downhill, so be prepared. There are more moose tracks than ski tracks in there.

Soon after the bridge, the trail winds up to meet Park Tote Road at Rocky Pond. A few yards before this, another trail, which leads to Round Pond, goes to the left.

Turn right on the wide Park Tote Road and climb. Compared with the ski trail, it's as wide as an interstate. Sledders may be on the rollercoaster of a road, which offers Katahdin views to one side, and later, views of Abol Pond on the other. Pass the entrances to the Abol Pond Scout Areas, which have lean-tos and picnic tables down by water's edge. Near the 4.0-mile mark, turn left at a familiar junction where you earlier crossed the Park Tote Road. The trail this way is a thriller of a zigzag along Abol Pond. Pop out by the Abol Beach Picnic Area junction, making a quick, quick right and left, or just go left to the beach. The trail now flattens out again and returns to the parking area the same way, again with those wondrous Katahdin views.

How to get there

The trailhead is about 20 miles from downtown Millinocket. From downtown Millinocket, at the light at Central and Penobscot, head straight on Central. At 0.1 mile, turn right at sign for Baxter State Park. At 0.3 mile, turn left at sign for Baxter State Park. This is Lake Road. Follow it about 9 miles as the plowing ends, then take a right on the Golden Road. Follow it 10 miles. Park in the unsigned area to the left, about 200 yards or so from the Abol Bridge.

The Bait Hole

Bait Hole Cross-Country Ski Trails, Millinocket, Maine

Type of trail:	▬▬ ▨
Distance:	3.0-mile loop (The Bait Hole); optional North Twin Dam Loop 2.0 miles, Beaver Pond Loop 1.1 miles
Terrain:	Flat to rolling hills with distant views over Elbow Lake to neighboring mountains, like Katahdin
Trail difficulty:	Easiest
Surface quality:	Groomed and tracked
Time:	1 hour
Food and facilities:	There aren't any facilities at the Bait Hole Trails, so if you need it, bring it. The trails are free. Donations are accepted in a box by the trailhead. Central Street in Millinocket has the necessary conveniences, including grocery stores and hotels. Off Central Street on Medway Road is the Hotel Terrace, which has all-you-can-eat breakfast and lunch buffets, so go before and after the ski. There are eleven rooms there too. The number is (207) 723–4525. The question of ski and snowshoe rentals should be put to the Katahdin Area Chamber of Commerce at (207) 723–4443. It's best to bring your own. The trails are not skate groomed, just classic. Many sections are double-wide, so that skiers can travel abreast. Snowshoers are welcome on all trails, but asked to stay off the ski tracks.
Phone numbers:	For Bait Hole Cross-Country Ski Trails conditions, call volunteer trailmaster Don Nodine at (207) 723–4329. The Katahdin Area Chamber of Commerce is at (207) 723–4443.

In the shadows of Maine's highest peak, Mount Katahdin, the Bait Hole Cross-Country Ski Trails are probably one of the state's most well-known secrets. Through the savvy work of area volunteers, some 6.0 miles of groomed trails wind along logging roads, access roads, and paths cut by the skiers themselves as part of the Millinocket Municipal Trail Network. The volunteers, skiing and snowshoeing members of the Northern Timber Cruisers Snowmobile Club, maintain the Bait Hole Trails and the 11.0 miles that are part of the Millinocket Area Cross-Country Ski Trails at the organization's clubhouse. The trails are linked by a flat-to-rolling 5.0-mile ski along the Golden Connector Trail. Some one-third of the club members are skier-only members.

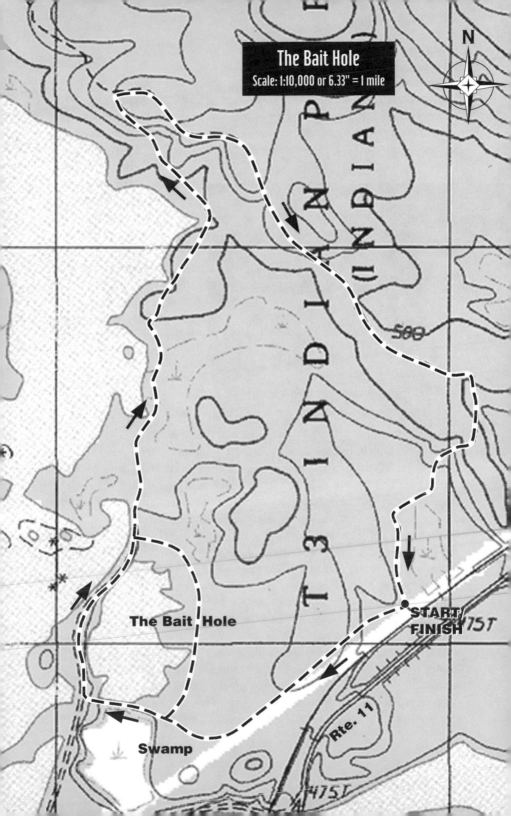

N

The Bait Hole
Scale: 1:10,000 or 6.33" = 1 mile

500

The Bait Hole

START/
FINISH

475 T

Swamp

Rte. 11

475 T

Millinocket and snowmobiling go hand in hand. The area has miles and miles of sled trails. The Bait Hole Trails provide a way for the skiers and snowshoers to enjoy distant mountain views in relative peace.

This is no-frills skiing. The Millinocket community has many early retirees: When paper company employees were offered early retirement, many took it. Now in winter, the trails are used by locals for midweek exercise, while visitors come on weekends and tend to fill the parking areas.

The Bait Hole is a popular ski in Millinocket.

One such resident, Don Nodine, has made the trails a passion. He cuts new ones, grooms the existing ones, and has mapped out both systems. In an effort to assuage skiers who don't like hills, Nodine and company cut bypasses so schussers can take the easy way out.

The system has numerous loop trails, offering shelter from the cold wind that blows down from the mountains and across Elbow Lake. There is actually a bypass trail, dubbed by locals as "No Wind Way," which takes skiers into the woods when the wind chills head for the South Pole. The system is largely flat, which makes it ideal for families and newcomers to the sports. There are some rolling hills, even a steep pitch or two, but the trails are wonderfully sheltered through the spruce, fir, birch, and poplar along the way.

The Bait Hole is the most popular way to get around the system. But a close second is the just under 2.0-mile North Twin Dam Loop. Skied counterclockwise, the loop skirts the area between the Bait Hole and a swamp, while heading to the dam with its fine views out across North Twin Lake, before ducking back into the woods and along the Penobscot River.

What's a bait hole? It's where area fishermen have gone to get tiny shiners to lure bigger fish. Now it's a popular ski. The loop officially begins at the signboard by the active railroad tracks used by the Bangor and Aroostook line. At the board, the system is mapped out and suggestions are made for loop trails. The network is well signed and mapped.

The Bait Hole Loop crosses the tracks and bears to the left, entering the woods on a small hill. The trail leads through the woods and after about 0.3 mile, it comes to a junction. On windy days, take a right. That's the "No Wind Way," a pleasant meander. Otherwise, stay straight and ski between the coves of Elbow Lake and the oblong Bait Hole, a small pond. Both ways eventually cross a series of dikes, which are beautiful places to get for far-reaching mountain views of peaks like rounded Jo-Mary Mountain and frosty Katahdin. Skiers do venture across the Bait Hole when the ice is thick enough. Skiing across the dikes is a beautiful experience, providing you with those water and mountain snapshots.

Directions at a glance

0.0 Enter woods from sign for Bait Hole Trail.

0.1 Cross B & A line train tracks and bear left.

0.4 Either turn right (on a windy day) or stay straight. Both trails cross a series of dikes and lead to the other side of the Bait Hole.

2.4 Turn right by sign to parking area 0.5 mile.

2.9 Cross train tracks and follow trail back to parking area.

Dip back into the woods and climb a bit. The Bait Hole Trail does a hard hairpin right as another trail goes off to Smith Pond. A few rolling hills lead to a place called "4 Corners." Got some zip, ski the 1.1-mile loop around the beaver pond from here. But roll back down, following the sign for the parking area, and come out by the Broken Arrow Archery Range (don't worry, they shoot in the fall), which leads right back to the train tracks.

How to get there

From Millinocket, travel on Route 11 south out of town. From the Bowater sign and entrance to Golden Road, it's 2.5 miles to the unsigned parking area on the left side. If that parking area is full, travel another 0.5 mile to the next one on the right. The trails to Bait Hole begin across the street from the first parking area.

Millinocket Area Cross-Country Ski Trails
Millinocket, Maine

Type of trail: ▬▬▬

Distance: 10.5-mile loop

Terrain: Narrow trails on mostly flat to gently rolling terrain

Trail difficulty: Easiest to more difficult

Surface quality: Groomed for classical

Time: 4 hours

Food and facilities: Rest rooms, water, and food can be found at the Northern Timber Cruisers Clubhouse on weekends, holidays, and during school vacation weeks. You'll find trail information inside the clubhouse, too. Twice a month the club has public suppers as fund-raisers, so if you time it right, eat hardy. When the clubhouse is closed, you're on your own, but a trail map is posted by the entrance to the A trail. A snowmobile museum is also on-site and basically has the same hours as the clubhouse. Though the trail system is free, donations are accepted at the clubhouse for the cross-country ski trails. A warming hut, located on the system, has a woodstove and places to sit. The question of ski and snowshoe rentals should be put to the Katahdin Area Chamber of Commerce. It's best to bring your own equipment. The trails are not skate groomed, just classic. For overnights, the chamber can help with accommodations at places like the Pamola on Central Street.

Phone numbers: For trail conditions, call volunteer trailmaster Don Nodine at (207) 723–4329. The Katahdin Area Chamber of Commerce is at (207) 723–4443.

Put cross-country skiing and snowmobiling together and what have you got?

An oxymoron.

At least that may be the view of some, but at the Northern Timber Cruisers Clubhouse in Millinocket, 11.0 miles of narrow, groomed ski trails make it so that both can coexist on a small swath of Bowater-Great Northern Paper's holdings in Maine. Located less than 2 miles from downtown Millinocket and just on the outskirts of Baxter State Park, the trails are part of a working forest. Skiers will see signs of loggers' harvests and no doubt will hear the occasional logging truck off in the distance. Then again, the system, like the Bait Hole network also overseen by the

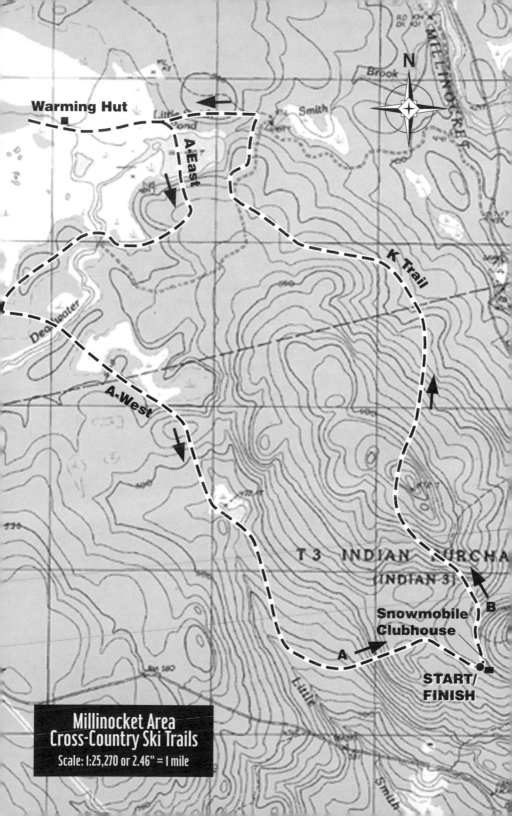

cross-country skiing members of the Northern Timber Cruisers, is no-frills and free.

Skate-skiers won't have room for their long strides on the easy, meandering trails found here. Handmade signs mark the way. Some are short spur trails that connect the three main trails—A-West, A-East, and K—that all loop together. As homage to those who have maintained the trails over the years, connector trails are named after them. Look for Harold's Sluice, Freddie's Freeway, and Shorty's Short-Cut.

The trails all loop around together. Toss a coin to figure out which is best. Some head up K and come down A-East for about a 9.0-mile loop. Others head up A-East and down K. Start on one, take a spur to the other. Use the C and A-West Trails as part of another loop. The choice is yours.

A-East, a mellow, gradually ascending jaunt to the warming hut, is thought to be the easiest way there. The trail includes a most stunning slice across the frozen white desert of Little Smith Pond. Either way, look for that Katahdin view. Also, A-East is sheltered. On those windy days, take it.

As for the K Trail, it is slightly more difficult than A-East. The trail also ascends gradually, has a nice roller, then softly cruises down for a spell, before heading out of the windproof forest and across a majestic opening that provides views of Katahdin to put a smile on anyone's face, regardless of how hard the wind may blow. By combining the K, A-East, C, and A-West Trails, skiers can put together a loop just over 10.0 miles and includes curves through the

Volunteers oversee the cross-country ski trails in Millinocket. At times, Katahdin can be spotted while skiing to the warming hut.

woods, Katahdin views, a stop at the warming hut, a ski across Little Smith Pond, a visit across a peat bog, and nice meandering downhills.

Though the individual trails are easy, the distance makes this trip a bit on the harder side of easy.

Directions at a glance

0.0 Leave via the K Trail found by a brown tool shed to the right of the A Trail, head northwest.

3.2 Stay straight as K merges with the A-East Trail.

4.7 Reach the warming hut. Leave the warming hut via the A-East Trail and follow it 1.5 miles, then right, across pond.

7.2 Turn right on the C Trail, heading for A-West.

8.2 Turn left on A-West southeast and follow it 2.3 miles back to the clubhouse.

Start on the K Trail, just beside the A Trail chute. Follow the K about 2.0 miles through the woods, before coming out to the Katahdin views. Dip into the woods a spell, and when you cross the bridge, it's only another 1.8 miles to the warming hut, along a mostly level ski through spruce and fir. At 3.2 miles, the K Trail joins up with the A-East, and in about 1.5 miles, you reach the warming hut. Head in, light the woodstove, sign the guest book and relax. Return to the clubhouse via the A-East Trail, taking it as it crosses Little Smith Pond. The trail comes to an intersection where the C Trail comes in on the right. Take the C Trail for a bit of everything. Katahdin can be spotted through the trees at times along this narrow and curvy trail. The C hands off to the A-West Trail. This trail too is a mixed bag of rollers and flats—with a curve or two thrown in for good measure. The trail skirts Little Smith Brook Pond and leads back to the clubhouse.

How to get there

From downtown Millinocket, at the intersection of Central and Penobscot, head straight on Central. At 0.1 mile, turn right at sign for Baxter State Park. At 0.3 mile, turn left at sign for Baxter State Park. This is Lake Road. At 1.7 mile, turn right at sign for Northern Timber Cruisers Clubhouse.

Mount Battie
Camden Hills State Park, Camden, Maine

Type of trail: ▬▬ 🟢

Also used by: Hikers

Distance: 1.0 mile round-trip (Mount Battie Trail) or 2.8 miles round-trip (Mount Battie Road)

Terrain: Short but hearty snowshoe to the top of Mount Battie and the stone tower, or more moderate ski or snowshoe via the auto road.

Trail difficulty: More difficult

Surface quality: Ungroomed

Time: 1 hour

Food and facilities: Bring your own water. Toilets are located near the stone tower on top of Mount Battie. There are also toilets and a pay phone by the toll station for those accessing the mountain via the Mount Battie Road. Picnic tables are also by the toll road entrance. Rentals can be had at Maine Sport Outfitters, Route 1, Rockport (207–236–7120 or 888–236–8797). Camden has supplies. There are grocery stores on Route 1, and the Camden Farmers Union, Mountain Street, is near the Mount Battie Trail parking area. The Waterfront Restaurant on Bay View Street (207–236–3747), Camden, is for the posttrek meal. The Cyder Valley Farm Bed and Breakfast (207–763–4478 or 877–899–0196), Youngtown Road, Lincolnville, is very comfortable (with views overlooking vineyards) and just a few miles from downtown Camden.

Phone numbers: Call Camden Hills State Park at (207) 236–3109. The Camden, Rockport, Lincolnville Chamber of Commerce is at (207) 236–4404 or (800) 223–5459. Like any trip to the coast of Maine in winter, always call ahead for snow conditions.

The Camden Hills are a tight cluster of mountains north of the coastal town of Camden. The highest is 1,380-foot Mount Megunticook. The mountain, like much of the range that has its name, is located within the 5,500 acres of Camden Hills State Park with its 30.0 miles of hiking and backcountry ski trails. Though Megunticook gets the prize for the being the tallest peak on the mainland Atlantic seaboard (Cadillac Mountain in Acadia is higher, but is on an island), it is the 800-foot-high Mount Battie that revels in popularity.

A stone tower is perched atop the open ledges. From it, the magnificent views extend from mountains to sea, from the steeples of Camden to the rolling countryside. The tower, with its spiral staircase, was erected in 1921 as a monument to local soldiers who fought in World War I. In the years around 1900, a hotel graced the summit of the mountain.

Mount Battie, on the park's south side, is reachable two ways: the Mount Battie Trail or the Mount Battie Road.

The 0.5-mile Mount Battie Trail is convenient to downtown Camden. It is not for skiers. From a small parking area, the blue-and-white blazed trail leaves the thin woods and nearly instantly provides views of Camden. The trek is moderate, and depending on the snowfall, it can be icy on the ledges. Cairns are also used to mark the way.

The trail begins at a moderate pace and increases in steepness in a few pitches along the ascent. Nearly halfway up, it reaches an open area with fine views, before heading back into the trees and up to the open summit of Mount Battie.

The unplowed Mount Battie Road is longer and not as steep. The road travels 1.4 miles to the summit. Snowshoers or skiers can use the wooded road, which also leads to the tower and loops around the summit. The road climbs gradually to the saddle between Mount Battie and Mount Megunticook before curving to the top. The gradual downhill back to the parking area is a pleasant ski.

> ## Directions at a glance
>
> **Mount Battie Trail**
>
> 0.0 Leave the parking area on the Mount Battie Trail going north and follow it 0.5 mile to the summit.
>
> 0.5 Summit and return.
>
> **Mount Battie Road**
>
> 0.0 Leave the parking area by the gated road and follow it to the west 1.4 miles to summit.
>
> 1.4 Reach summit and return.

How to get there

For the Mount Battie Trail, take Route 52 (Mountain Street) from the junction with Route 1 in Camden. Turn right onto Megunticook Street and follow it to the end where there is a parking lot.

For the Mount Battie Road, from the junction of Routes 52 and Route 1, bear right on Route 1 for about 1.5 miles. Turn left on unsigned road by ranger house.

Ducktrap River Loop
Tanglewood 4-H Camp and Learning Center, Lincolnville, Maine

Type of trail: ▬▬▬ ⬤

Distance: 4.6-mile loop

Terrain: Rolling terrain along river bank, which features a stop at a suspension bridge

Trail difficulty: Easiest

Surface quality: Ungroomed

Time: 1½ hours skiing, 4½ hours snowshoeing

Food and facilities: Bring your own water. There are no toilets. A shelter is found just off the loop. Rentals can be had at Maine Sport Outfitters, Route 1, Rockport (207–236–7120 or 888–236–8797). Camden has supplies, though there is a convenience store on Route 1 in Lincolnville Beach. The Whales Tooth Pub and Restaurant, Route 1, Lincolnville Beach (207–789–5200), has incredible fish and chips. The Cyder Valley Farm Bed and Breakfast (207–763–4478 or 877–899–0196), Youngtown Road, Lincolnville, is very comfortable with views overlooking their vineyards and is off the beaten path.

Phone numbers: Tanglewood 4-H Camp and Learning Center is (207) 789–5868. The Camden, Rockport, Lincolnville Chamber of Commerce is (207) 236–4404 or (800) 223–5459.

Nearly 10.0 miles of trails run through the Tanglewood 4-H Camp and Learning Center's Cross-Country Ski Area. The eight trails wind through the evergreen forest, leading down to the banks of the Black Brook and Ducktrap River. Wide and smooth, or narrow and bumpy, the trail system provides no-frills skiing just miles from the Atlantic in midcoast Maine.

A group of volunteers oversee the operation of the system. The 4-H Camp is run by the University of Maine Cooperative Extension, Knox-Lincoln County office. These trails are not patrolled, nor are they groomed. On occasion the Camden/Rockport High School will use portions of the network for races, and the race loop will be groomed.

Many neat and solid wooden bridges are scattered across the several brooks and rivers on the property. They are easy to negotiate. Also, a wooden suspension bridge spans the Ducktrap River. The flowing river, bridge, and encapsulated feeling of the forest make for a unique destination. The ski along the banks of the Ducktrap River is a pleasurable out-

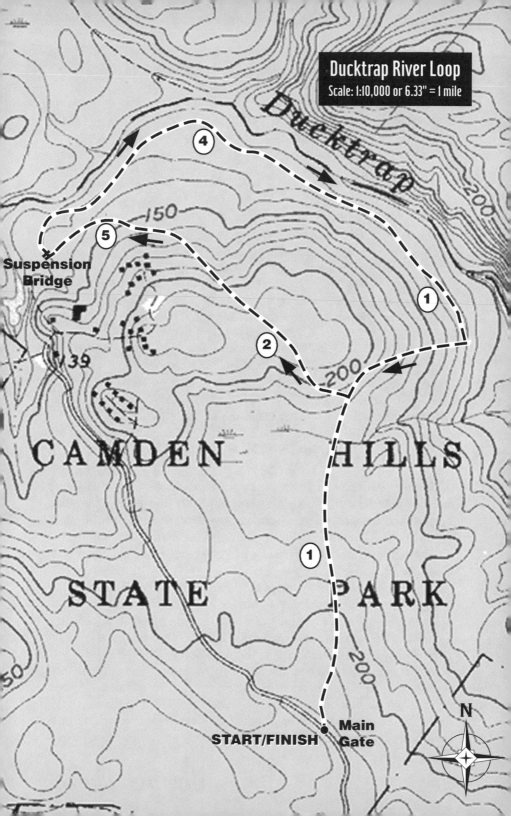

ing, the trail sometimes follows the bank and sometimes leaves its edge only to come back. A shelter just off the trail, overlooking the river, is a nice lunch spot, but so is the river's edge itself.

The system is by no means flat. Rustic in nature with well-placed wooden signs along the way (maps are available in the mailbox at the trailhead), a few of the trails are hilly with steep pitches thrown in. The trails aren't named, just numbered. No pets are allowed on the trails, with the exception of Trail 8, the Old Whitney Road. The 1.0-mile-long trail is also used by snowmobiles. Also, snowmobiles might use Tanglewood Road to the suspension bridge.

There are several loop trips on the property. The high school race team uses Trail 1, a 3.5-mile loop with a steep narrow drop thrown in. The 1.5-mile-long loop along Trail 6 takes skiers along both the Black Brook and Ducktrap River.

At nearly 4.0 miles long, a loop incorporating Trails 1, 2, 5, and 4 takes skiers into the forest along the river. Trail 1 is basically level to rolling at the onset, slicing through on a wide swatch through the forest. Encounter the first of the many bridges just before the junction with Trail 2, a 0.3-mile connecting trail with a small, gradual uphill. Trail 5 then leads down to the suspension bridge, a bit of a rolling ride. Signs warn you to cross the bridge at your own risk.

The ski continues down to the banks of the river via Trail 4, playing a bit of a cat-and-mouse game with the river, crawling along the edge, then rising up above. The trail crosses many bridges. The shelter is by the junction with Trail 1. Ski along the river a bit more before taking a hard right and heading up a hill, away from the water's edge. Trail 1 eventually leads back to the parking area.

Directions at a glance

0.0 Leave parking area and walk or ski 200 yards to trailhead with Trail 1 on left. Head north on trail.

1.0 Turn left on Trail 2.

1.3 Bear right on Trail 5.

1.8 Reach suspension bridge. Ski back along Trail 5 for several hundred feet and bear left on Trail 4.

3.1 Stay straight on Trail 1.

3.3 Bear left on Trail 1. Bear right on Trail 1 and ski 1.0 mile south back to the parking area.

How to get there

From Camden, travel on Route 1 north to Lincolnville Beach. About 0.8 mile past Lincolnville Beach, turn left on Ducktrap Road. Travel 0.7 mile to first dirt road on right, Tanglewood Road, and turn right. Drive about 0.8 mile to parking area.

Ragged Mountain

Georges Highland Path, Rockport, Maine

Type of trail:	(icon)
Also used by:	Hikers
Distance:	5 miles round-trip
Terrain:	Moderate snowshoe to mountain views of Camden Hills and ocean
Trail difficulty:	More difficult
Surface quality:	Ungroomed
Time:	5 hours
Food and facilities:	Bring your own water. There are no rest rooms. Supplies can be had in Rockport. Rentals can be had at Maine Sport Outfitters, Route 1, Rockport (207–236–7120 or 888–236–8797). The Market Basket (207–236–4371), on Route 1 at the junction with Route 90 has last-minute items and sandwiches for after the trip. The chamber of commerce can help with accommodations. The Cyder Valley Farm Bed and Breakfast (207–763–4478 or 877–899–0196), Youngtown Road, Lincolnville, is very comfortable.
Phone numbers:	The Camden, Rockport, Lincolnville Chamber of Commerce is at (207) 236–4404 or (800) 223–5459. Call the Georges River Land Trust at (207) 594–5166. A map of the Ragged Mountain section is available from the Georges River Land Trust, 328 Main Street, Rockland, Maine 04841.

To snowshoe Ragged Mountain in Rockport is to be treated to commanding vistas of lakes, mountains, and the ocean. At 1,300 feet, the hulking mountain appears daunting as you gaze up at the huge boulders and rocky outcrops from the trailhead. But save for one moderate stretch up an old horse trail, the outing is a fairly easy undertaking to treasured views of the coast of Maine along a simple, well-marked path.

The 2.5-mile trail to the 1,225-foot point on the mountain—just shy of its summit—is called the Ragged Mountain section of the Georges Highland Path. The trail is still relatively new, opened in the fall of 1997.

Directions at a glance

0.0 Leave the parking area and follow the blue blazes of the trail north. Follow winding trail to summit.

2.5 Reach high point of Ragged Mountain. Return via same trail to parking area.

And the trail is still growing.

In 1987, a group of citizens formed the Georges River Land Trust, a group dedicated to protecting the 225 square miles of the hills, farms, and miles of the Saint Georges River watershed from Port Clyde to Frye Mountain in Montville. The nonprofit organization was also instrumental in establishing bikeways through the area and has plans for other trails. If all goes as planned, one day a four-season footpath will extend from Thomaston to Frye Mountain, a roughly 50-mile pathway with several spurs and loops.

A snowshoer heads downhill.

The Ragged Mountain section of the Georges Highland Path runs 9.0 miles from the base of Meadow Mountain, along Pleasant Mountain, over Spruce Mountain, and up Ragged Mountain. The trail up Ragged is but one section of the path.

The blue-blazed trail leaves the Route 17 parking area by a signboard, down a few steps, and then begins to wind its way through the woods. The trail affords occasional views of Ragged through the trees, and several times passes old stone walls, reminders of the early settlers who once lived in the shadow of the mountain, which now has a radio tower on its summit.

The trail is somewhat flat, with the occasional rise, passing through the oak, maple, and birch stands. The path loops hard to the right, passing by several wetlands, then following the base of the mountain. Huge boulders line the sides of the mountain at the foot of the slope. The trail then bends sharply to the left and begins the moderate climb up the old horse trail to a flat area lined with boulders. The trail rises above Mirror Lake and offers views of Mirror Lake and Spruce Mountain as it climbs along a ridge, giving a razorback feeling. You pass unobstructed views out to the rounded humps of Spruce, Pleasant, and Meadow Mountains. Mirror Lake is to the left, Grassy Pond to the right, in the distance.

The trail breaks out of the trees several times, crossing open rocky ledges where cairns blaze the way. Snowshoes with crampons are best to navigate the ledges, which could be sheathed in ice. From the ledges, you can spot Mount Battie, the coast, the rolling countryside, lakes, and mountains.

One final push along the rocky section leads to a sign, just below the radio tower, which marks the high point of the Ragged Mountain Trail, some 1,225 feet above sea level.

How to get there

From Rockport and the junction of Routes 1 and 90, turn right on Route 90, traveling west for 2.7 miles. Then turn right on Route 17 west. The parking area is 1.8 miles down the road on the right hand side by a yellow gate.

Around Mountain Loop

Packman Mountain, Acadia National Park, Bar Harbor, Maine

Type of trail:	▬▬▬
Distance:	11.0-mile loop
Terrain:	Beautiful rolling terrain around three peaks with ocean, lake, and mountain views. One long moderate climb.
Trail difficulty:	More difficult
Surface quality:	Skier tracked though portions are groomed by volunteers at times.
Time:	4 hours
Food and facilities:	There is a toilet at the Parkman Mountain trailhead. Bring your own water. Cross-country ski and snowshoe rentals can be had from Cadillac Mountain Sports on Cottage Street in nearby Bar Harbor (207–288–4532). Winter camping is offered in Acadia National Park year-round at the Blackwoods camping area. For those who prefer the indoors, the Mill Brook House Bed and Breakfast, 59 Old Norway Drive, Bar Harbor (207–288–3860), is quiet and comfortable. Cottage Street in Bar Harbor is also the place for groceries. Main Street has Galyn's Restaurant for a well-deserved dinner.
Phone numbers:	Acadia National Park headquarters can be reached by calling (207) 288–3338. The Bar Harbor Chamber of Commerce is at (800) 288–5103.

The twin rounded peaks of South and North Bubbles rim the long and lovely Jordan Pond. From a vantage point high up the side of a mountain, gaze out to unobstructed views of Somes Sound. Cross seven stone bridges. This is the Around Mountain Loop.

The 11.0-mile circuit is the longest loop in the carriage road system

and offers skiers exciting vistas along with a workout. On this circuit, skiers get a chance to see the impact that the wind and sun have on the carriage roads. Be prepared for windswept snows as the carriage road ascends the mountains.

There is more than one mountain on this Around Mountain Loop. The most prominent peaks are the 1,323-foot Sargent, 1,194-foot Penobscot, and 941-foot Parkman.

Around Mountain Loop begins at the Parkman Mountain trailhead, climbing immediately. Just follow the numbered carriage road intersections. The beauty of the carriage roads is immediately obvious as the road darts in and out of the trees, allowing views of the lakes down below. The long, moderate climb winds upward for a couple of miles. Initially though, there are a few steep and winding pitches. As the road rises, it leaves the trees behind. The wind may pick up as the hulking mountains take center stage. Look down to see the carriage roads beneath you. Mountains, lakes, and the sea are all part of the stunning scenery you'll see when the road breaks out from the shelter of the forest.

Near the 3.4-mile mark, cross the first of the stone bridges, Chasm Brook Bridge. At Intersection 10, roll down into a very beautiful piece of the planet. Giant rocks and cliffs line one side of the path, and Jordan Pond, ringed by mountains, sits on the other. The ski continues downward at this point, but be sure to stop to admire the scenery. Large blocks of granite line the roads. They served as guardrails for the system.

The wide and winding carriage roads of Acadia National Park are ideal for skiing and snowshoeing.

The rocks, dubbed Rockefeller's Teeth, aren't spaced at regular intervals. The signposts are made of cedar. Carriage drivers once used them for directions. In winter, skiers and snowshoers still use them.

The road swings downward, leaves the lakeside, and heads back into the forest cover. The road rolls along at this point and passes several vantage points that offer vistas and places for reflection along the bridges. Amphitheater Bridge, at about 7.7 miles into the trip, takes the skier into a boxlike canyon. The bridge is the longest span of the bridges by Rockefeller, at 236 feet.

What goes up, goes down, and the loop's rollercoaster feel continues until the final, at times winding, descent to the trailhead.

Directions at a glance

0.0	Leave Parkman Mountain trailhead and turn right on carriage road.
0.1	Reach Intersection 13 and bear left.
0.3	Reach Intersection 12 and turn left.
3.9	Reach Intersection 10 and bear right.
6.0	Reach Intersection 14 and turn right.
7.0	Reach Intersection 21 and bear right.
8.2	Reach Intersection 20 and bear right.
9.1	Reach Intersection 19 and turn right.
10.8	Reach Intersection 12 and bear left.
11.0	Reach Intersection 13 and bear right.
11.1	Turn left into parking area.

How to get there

Take I–95 north to exit 45A, then I–395 east to exit 6A. Travel on Route 1A to Ellsworth and then Route 3 east to Bar Harbor. From intersection of Routes 3 and 233, bear right on Route 233 going west to junction with Routes 3/198. Turn left on Route 198 south and travel 2.5 miles to Parkman Mountain trailhead on left.

Eagle Lake

Acadia National Park, Bar Harbor, Maine

Type of trail:	▬▬▬ ⬭
Also used by:	Walkers
Distance:	6.0-mile loop
Terrain:	Gentle lake loop along famed Acadia National Park carriage roads
Trail difficulty:	Easiest
Surface quality:	Skier tracked though part is groomed by volunteers at times.
Time:	2 hours skiing, 6 hours snowshoeing
Food and facilities:	There are portable toilets at the Eagle Lake trailhead off Route 233. Park headquarters are located about 0.5 mile west of that. Water is available there. Cross-country ski and snowshoe rentals can be had from Cadillac Mountain Sports on Cottage Street in nearby Bar Harbor (207–288–4532). Winter camping is offered in Acadia National Park year-round at the Blackwoods camping area. For those who prefer the indoors, the Mill Brook House Bed and Breakfast, 59 Old Norway Drive, Bar Harbor (207–288–3860), is quiet and comfortable. Cottage Street in Bar Harbor is also the place for groceries. Main Street has Geddy's for that après-ski gastronomic adventure.
Phone numbers:	Acadia National Park headquarters can be reached by calling (207) 288–3338. The Bar Harbor Chamber of Commerce is at (800) 288–5103.

Thanks to a Rockefeller, skiers and snowshoers now have about 50 miles of rustic carriages roads to glide around the mountains and lakes of Maine's Acadia National Park. Philanthropist John D. Rockefeller Jr. was a skilled equestrian. He desired motor-free paths into the heart of Mount Desert Island. For twenty seven years, from 1913 to 1940, his construction efforts resulted in roads with sweeping ocean vistas.

These roads of broken stone that wind through the eastern half of the island, past lakes and mountains, are now enjoyed by travelers year-round.

Gently graded and lined with gravel, the carriage roads are somewhat mazelike but well marked. They offer the winter recreationalist a chance to glide over handsome stone bridges and through the woods.

The history of Maine's national park goes back long before a Rockefeller was born. Artifacts indicate Indian encampments dating back 6,000

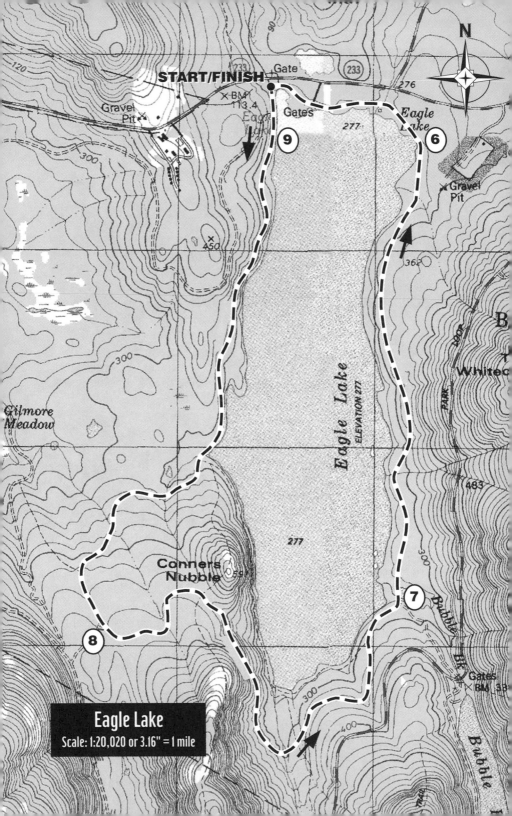

START/FINISH

Eagle Lake
Scale: 1:20,020 or 3.16" = 1 mile

From the carriage roads in Acadia National Park, the vistas are forever changing and worthwhile.

years. The first written descriptions of Maine coast Native Americans describe people who lived off the land by hunting, fishing, and gathering plants and berries. The Abenakis know Mount Desert Island as "the sloping land."

It wasn't until the mid-1800s that wealthy visitors like the Rockefellers, Morgans, Fords, Vanderbilts, Carnegies, and Astors chose to summer on the island. They would congregate at elegant estates, which they called cottages, and enjoy ostentatious gatherings.

Winter is a quieter time on Mount Desert Island. Bar Harbor isn't bustling. The scenic 27.0-mile Park Loop Road within Acadia isn't fully opened. However, it can be used by snowshoers, skiers, and snowmobilers. And the highest peak on the island, Cadillac at 1,530 feet, is a commanding sight.

The island isn't blessed with much natural snowfall. Only about 60 inches falls annually. But when it does snow, the 16-foot-wide carriage roads are a pleasure to explore. All the miles are not tracked and groomed. A nonprofit watchdog group called the Friends of Acadia grooms certain sections of the roads when 4 inches of snow falls. It is absolutely imperative to call Acadia before making the trip to make sure there is snow. Even in midwinter, the carriage roads can be cordoned off because the roads become muddy.

Park volunteers—Friends of Acadia—groom various sections of the roads, like Eagle Lake, Witch Hole Pond, Aunt Betty Pond, Upper Hadlock Loop, Parkman Mountain to Gilmore Meadow, and Gilmore Meadow to Jordan Pond.

Two of the most popular loops leave from the same trailhead on Route 233—Eagle Lake and Witch Hole Pond.

The second largest lake on the island, Eagle Lake is untattered by shoreline development. Instead, mountains like Cadillac, North and South Bubbles, Pemetic, and Sargent ring the 436-acre lake. The nearly 6.0-mile loop, taken counterclockwise, begins at the Eagle Lake trailhead and immediately goes under one of the stone bridges. Skiers first ski gradually up the west side of the lake, winding along the shoreline. You can see Eagle Lake through the trees.

Directions at a glance

0.0 Leave the trailhead, turning left and crossing under the bridge.

0.1 At Intersection 9, stay straight.

2.0 Reach Intersection 8 and bear left.

3.8 Reach Intersection 7 and bear left.

5.8 Reach Intersection 6 and turn right under bridge, then right again into parking area.

But it is on the eastern side that skiers can enjoy a nice, long descent and some of the finer views of the mountains and lake, as the ski wraps up back at the trailhead.

How to get there

Take I–95 north to exit 45A, then I–395 east to exit 6A. Travel on Route 1A to Ellsworth and then Route 3 east to Bar Harbor. From intersection of Routes 3 and 233, bear right on Route 233, going west for approximately 3 miles to Eagle Lake trailhead on right.

Witch Hole Pond

Acadia National Park, Bar Harbor, Maine

Type of trail: ▬▬▬ ⬭

Distance: 5.5-mile or 7.0-mile loop

Terrain: Flat to rolling with a trek up Paradise Hill to ocean views

Trail difficulty: Easiest to more difficult

Surface quality: Skier tracked though groomed by volunteers at times

Time: 2½ hours skiing

Food and facilities: There are portable toilets at the Eagle Lake trailhead off Route 233. Park headquarters are located about 0.5 mile west of that. Water is available there. Cross-country ski and snowshoe rentals can be had from Cadillac Mountain Sports on Cottage Street in nearby Bar Harbor (207–288–4532). Winter camping is offered in Acadia National Park year-round at the Blackwoods camping area. For those who prefer the indoors, the Mill Brook House Bed and Breakfast, 59 Old Norway Drive, Bar Harbor (207–288–3860) is quiet and comfortable. Cottage Street in Bar Harbor is also the place for groceries. Main Street has Geddy's for that après-ski meal.

Phone numbers: Acadia National Park headquarters can be reached by calling (207) 288–3338. The Bar Harbor Chamber of Commerce is at (800) 288–5103.

Acadia National Park is where mountains, lakes, and the sea come together on heart-shaped Mount Desert Island. A short bridge connects the island to the mainland. Seventeen mountains are on the island, ranging in elevation from 200 to 1,530 feet, according to the Appalachian Mountain Club's hiking bible, the *AMC Maine Mountain Guide*.

Though the island's hiking trails can be somewhat hilly and downright vertical (the ladders on the Precipice and Beehive Trails come to mind), it can also be smooth. That's where the carriage roads around Witch Hole Pond come in to play.

The Eagle Lake trailhead off Route 233 (Eagle Lake Road) has some of the easiest snowshoeing and cross-country skiing in the park. Witch Pond Hole, by throwing in the moderate ups and downs of Paradise Hill, is nearly a 7.0-mile circuit. Skiers can, if they wish, bypass Paradise Hill and just ski or snowshoe 5.5 miles. But Paradise Hill is aptly named. The ocean views out to Hulls Cove and Frenchman Bay are outstanding. The rocky shores of the island are what attracted French explorer Samuel de

Champlain. He is credited with discovering and naming the island when he ran aground there in 1604. Frenchman Bay was a spot where French ships hid from British ships during the French and Indian War.

Skiers and snowshoers begin the trek from the Eagle Lake trailhead and turn right at the first junction. The carriage road is basically flat on this part of the journey and will pass Breakneck Ponds before reaching the signposts at Intersection 4. Turning left, the road skirts Halfmoon Pond and reaches the waters of Witch Hole Pond in about 1.0 mile. It is at Intersection 2 that you must make a choice. If you want to do the shorter 5.5-mile loop, turn right. But if you are seeking glorious vistas, turn left and ascend Paradise Hill.

Directions at a glance

0.0 Leave Eagle Lake trailhead and turn right, following signs for Witch Hole Pond.

1.1 Reach Intersection 4 and turn left.

2.1 Reach Intersection 2 and stay straight or turn right to Intersection 3 for the shorter 5.5-mile route, which by-passes Paradise Hill.

2.3 Reach Intersection 1 and bear right.

3.7 Reach Intersection 3 and bear left.

5.7 Reach Intersection 4 and turn left.

After admiring the sea continue around the loop, bearing left at Intersection 3. In about 1.0 mile or so, look for the triple arches of the Duck Brook Bridge. The ski then rolls along back to Intersection 4, where a left will lead back past Breakneck Ponds and eventually to the familiar trailhead.

How to get there

Take I–95 north to exit 45A, then I–395 east to exit 6A. Travel on Route 1A to Ellsworth and then Route 3 east to Bar Harbor. From intersection of Routes 3 and 233, bear right on Route 233, heading west for approximately 3.0 miles to Eagle Lake trailhead on right.

Quaggy Jo Mountain Trail
Aroostook State Park, Presque Isle, Maine

Type of trail: ▰▰ ⬬

Also used by: Snowmobilers

Distance: 5.0-mile loop

Terrain: Rolling hills with 0.5-mile spur trail to the top of Quaggy Jo's north peak offer views into the surrounding hills and countryside of Maine's northernmost county.

Trail difficulty: Most difficult

Surface quality: Tracked as needed; usually after snow.

Time: 2 hours skiing, 5 hours snowshoeing

Food and facilities: Presque Isle has conveniences and supplies along Main Street (Route 1). Snowshoe rentals can be had at Aroostook Bicycle and Sport, 690 Main Street, Presque Isle (207–764–0206). The University of Maine's Outdoor Adventure Program International at Presque Isle also has rentals (207–768–9669). The Governor's Restaurant, 350 Main Street (207–769–2274), is a good spot after the trek. The chamber of commerce can help with overnights, and there is the Budget Traveler Motor Lodge on Main Street (800–958–0111). A small fee is charged for using the park. Toilets are available by the ski map at the far end of the parking area. You will find picnic tables by the lake's edge. There is no drinking water.

Phone numbers: Aroostook State Park can be reached by calling (207) 768–8341. The Presque Isle Chamber of Commerce is at (207) 764–6561. Aroostook County Tourism is (888) 216–2463.

Aroostook County runs along Maine's north and northwestern border. Synonymous with potatoes, and there are miles and miles of snow-covered fields, the county is larger than the area of Rhode Island and Connecticut put together. With 6,453 square miles, the county sprawls along the border with Atlantic Canada. It is, as they say, up there.

Presque Isle, in the central section of Aroostook, is home to, among other things, a University of Maine campus and the first state park in Maine. In 1938, interested residents of the community gave the state one hundred acres of land with the idea of starting a state park. One year later, that idea became a reality with the creation of Aroostook State Park. Now more than 600 acres, the park takes in Echo Lake and Quaggy Jo Mountain, the park's most distinctive landmark.

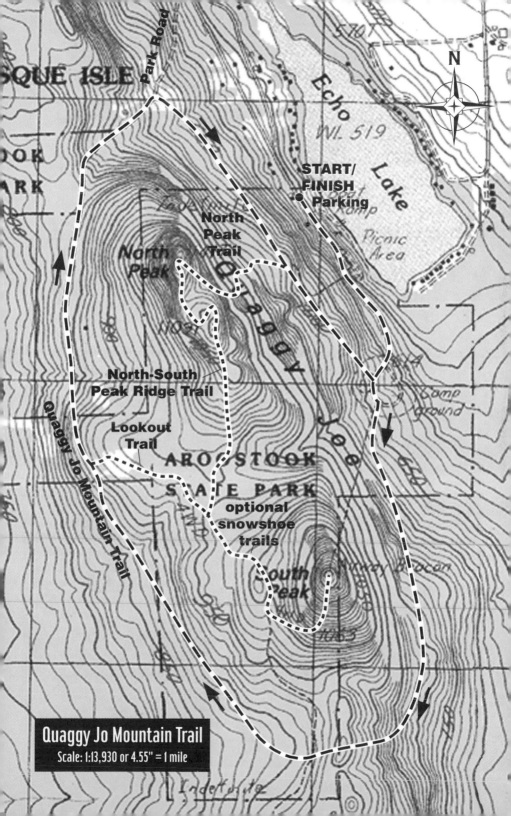

N

SQUE ISLE

OOK ARK

Park Road

Echo Lake

Wl. 519

START/
FINISH
Parking

North
Peak
Trail

North
Peak

Quaggy Jo

Picnic
Area

North-South
Peak Ridge Trail

Lookout
Trail

AROOSTOOK

STATE PARK

optional
snowshoe
trails

South
Peak

Quaggy Jo Mountain Trail

Camp
ground

Quaggy Jo Mountain Trail
Scale: 1:13,930 or 4.55" = 1 mile

Rising from the farms in the southwestern edge of Presque Isle, Quaggy Jo tops out at 1,213 feet. It rises some 600 feet above Echo Lake and has two peaks—north and south. The views of the surrounding

farms and hills are better from the north peak. Actually, the mountain itself traces its name back to the Native Americans who dubbed it *QuaQuaJo*. One translation given is "twin peaked."

Some 15 miles of cross-country ski trails wind through the park and on to adjacent private lands. Snowshoers can use the trails as long as they stay off the tracks. However, it might be best if visiting the park for

Aroostook State Park offers ski and snowshoe trails for all abilities.

snowshoers to stick to the hiking trails. A popular snowshoeing trail to the top of the northern peak is the 1.25-mile blue-blazed North Peak Trail through the conifers and hardwoods. From the North Peak summit, snowshoers can continue on to the south peak via the 1.0-mile North-South Peak Ridge Trail. The most popular route for snowshoeing though is up and down via the North Peak Trail.

Skiers can also reach the top of the northern peak with a spur trail off the exhilarating Quaggy Jo Mountain Trail. The 4.0-mile loop encircles the mountain through beech, fir, maple, and spruce. The circuit is for advanced skiers. Other skiers will find much to do at the park. At the far end of the parking lot, there is a ski trail map. From there, beginner skiers can try the mellow, blue-blazed Novice and Maze Trails, each 1.0 mile long. A step above are the Cedar and Sheep Trails. The 1.5-mile Sheep Trail meanders along the edge of an old sheep farm.

At Aroostook State Park, skiers are warned of the terrain ahead by "Gasp" Hill, part of the Quaggy Jo Mountain Trail.

But the gem of Aroostook is the Quaggy Jo Mountain Trail with its rolling hills, access to the north peak, and a downhill called "Gasp Hill." There are a couple of spur trails off Quaggy Jo, notably the 2.0-mile Maple Trail, which can extend the ski. The flat 0.5-mile Old Beacon Trail has nice views to the west.

Directions at a glance

0.0 Leave the parking area by the trail closest to the park entrance.

0.3 Turn right by campsite 18.

2.0 Turn right for Lookout Trail or stay straight on Quaggy Jo.

3.7 Bear left by campsite 3 and return to parking area.

The Quaggy Jo Mountain Trail twice crosses snowmobile trails. There is plenty of signage. The trail also has a rather exhilarating downhill, called "Gasp." This is because of the severe hard right turn near the bottom of a pitch. Now that you have been forewarned, there should be no surprises.

The trail leaves the near end of the parking lot and is unsigned. But just a few yards up the hill on the nice wide double-tracked trail, pass a sign for the nature trail and soon enter the campground. The trail bears to the right by campsite 18. The route is well signed with maps and markings. The trail rises moderately through the woods and passes several hiking paths. The first snowmobile junction is just after the junction with the Maple Trail. Here the trail begins a playful roll through the forest; once again, it passes another junction with the Maple Trail and another snowmobile crossing. The spur path up the Lookout Trail, about midway through the loop, is a good one to take. The trail is a flat grade initially, swings to the left and begins a moderate grade, and then is steep up to the top of the north peak. When it's icy, use caution. Otherwise, enjoy those Aroostook views and descend with abandon back to the Quaggy Jo Mountain Trail. The Quaggy Jo has its nice down descents, and it's about time for one. The trail passes a junction with the Old Beacon Trail, which leaves left. Then it's "Gasp" time. There's a sign. Zip on down, make that right, roll back up, and then wind through the woods before coming out by campsite 3. Bear left on the descent back into the campground and roll back down to the parking area.

How to get there

From Presque Isle, follow the signs to Aroostook State Park off Route 1 by turning onto the unsigned Spragueville Road. Follow it one mile and turn left on the State Park Road. The park entrance is about one mile down and the parking area is just ahead.

Lonesome Pine Trails
Fort Kent, Maine

Type of trail: ▬▬ ◄ ⊙

Distance: 3.0-mile loop

Terrain: Rolling hills open up to a vista locals call the "Top of the World."

Trail difficulty: More difficult

Surface quality: Groomed for skate and classical

Time: 1 hour skiing, 3 hours snowshoeing

Food and facilities: Cross-country ski and snowshoe rentals can be had from the ski shop at the Lonesome Pine Trails Ski Lodge off Hall Street. Its hours are Wednesday noon to 10:00 P.M., Friday 3:00 to 10:00 P.M., and Saturday and Sunday 9:00 A.M. to 4:00 P.M. Water and rest rooms are available at the ski lodge, where there is a cafe for snacks. At the warming hut on Fort Kent Village Road, there is only a toilet. Small trail fee. After the ski, go where the locals go, Rock's Diner, 91 West Main Street. For overnights, try the Fort Kent Motel, 66 West Main Street, Fort Kent (207–834–5725).

Phone numbers: Lonesome Pine Trails can be reached by calling (207) 834–5202.

It only seems fitting that a cross-country ski loop in the northeastern most corner of the United States be called "Top of the World." That's the unofficial name, but it certainly fits.

Fort Kent is a lively community of about 4,600 residents with an extremely active cross-country core. Fort Kent Community High School has been state Nordic champions many times over. Throw in an avid bunch of Nordic skiers in the Green Bean Ski Club and the trails at the base of a downtown ski area—Lonesome Pine Trails—and you've got about 15.0 miles of groomed trails in the heart of the community.

Fort Kent, called the gateway to the Allagash, also serves up fine international views on the trails. The town is found in Upper Saint John Valley, where the Saint John River is the natural boundary between Maine and New Brunswick, Canada. A French-Acadian culture thrives in the north of Maine, and the hint of French can be heard among the residents. Though you don't need a passport to get into Fort Kent, it sure seems you are in another world.

The network has two trailheads that provide access to pleasing views of the St. John and Fish River Valleys. One trailhead is at the Lonesome

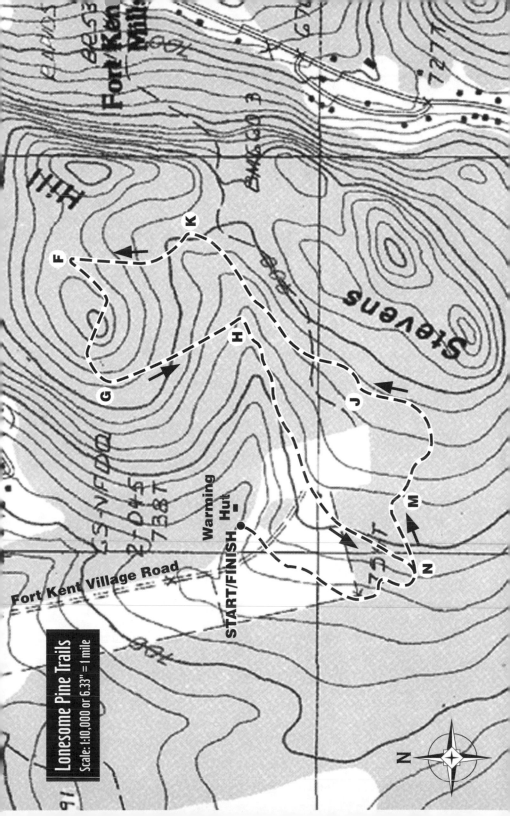

Well-marked trails make it easy for skiers to stay on the trail in Fort Kent.

Pine Trails Ski Lodge. From there, skiers can try the more challenging trails of the network. The high school team trains at the trails and competes on the 3.0-mile, hilly race loop accessed near the ski lodge.

Easier trails are found at the trailhead by the warming hut (built in 1997) on Front Kent Village Road. Trails on the west side of the hut are groomed with two classical tracks. These trails wind through the woods, and there is a very gentle 5.0-mile loop that beginner skiers can do. East of the hut is where one classical track is set and a skate lane is groomed. That's where the "Top of the World Loop" can be found.

As a side note, skiers can also access the "Top of the World Loop" from the ski lodge by taking the T-bar to the top of the ski hill. Inquire at the ski lodge for more information.

There are numerous intersections on the trails from the warming hut. There are orange signs at the lettered junctions, which are used in conjunction with post maps. So it's fairly easy to ski from lettered junction to junction and know where you are. There aren't really trail names, just numbers. But, the trailblazers do pay homage to local skiers by naming certain areas of the network, like Jamie's Jump and Lucien's Lillehammer, after them. The "Top of the World" circuit follows Trails 5 and 4 from the warming hut. It is very wide and well maintained with lots of rolling hills. There are at least three snowmobile trail crossings.

The ski begins outside the warming hut and goes through the cedar woods. The wide flat trail soon starts a moderate climb as it rises along a ridge and leaves the woods at a scenic vista dubbed "Top of the World." You see rounded hills from the overlook

Directions at a glance

0.0 Leave the warming hut on Trail 5 and head south.

0.3 Reach Junction N, turn left on Trail 5.

0.6 Reach Junction M, bear right on Trail 5.

0.9 Reach Junction J, bear right on Trail 4.

1.5 Reach Junction K, turn left on Trail 4.

1.8 Reach Junction F, turn left on Trail 4, following it to the left, past Junction G.

2.3 Reach Junction H, bear right on Trail 5, and follow back to warming hut.

before you duck back into the forest. The course now is like a dragon's tail with rolling trails, curves, and flat spots. The circuit winds through the woods, offering some nice downhills. When the signs start pointing to the X-C Warming Hut, just follow them back.

How to get there

For the Lonesome Pine Trails Ski Lodge, follow Route 161 north from Caribou to Fort Kent. From West Main Street, turn left on Hall Street and follow it to the top. Bear left at the junction into the ski area parking lot.

For the Fort Kent Village Road warming hut, follow Route 161 north from Caribou to Fort Kent. From West Main Street, pass the municipal offices and in about 0.25 mile, then turn left on Fort Kent Village Road. Follow it 1.0 mile to the parking area on the right.

The Border Trail

Mars Hill, Maine

Type of trail:	⬤ , ▬▬▬ (portions)
Also used by:	Hikers
Distance:	7.2 miles one way from Bigrock Ski Lodge to U. S. Customs office; trail can also be accessed at U. S. Customs office or mid-way via Knoxford Road
Terrain:	Climb steeply up Mars Hill, then roll down to the Canadian border on a trail bisecting two countries.
Trail difficulty:	More difficult
Surface quality:	Ungroomed
Time:	7 hours
Food and facilities:	Cross-country ski and snowshoe rentals are available from Ski City, Fort Street, Mars Hill (207–425–7147). The University of Maine's Outdoor Adventure Program International at Presque Isle also has rentals (207–768–9669). In the Bigrock Ski Area base lodge, you'll find toilets, water, and food. On the south peak of Mars Hill is a shelter for overnights. There is a pit toilet out back. Nearby Presque Isle has hotels, like the Northeastland Hotel on Main Street (207–768–5321). After the trek, choose from several restaurants in Presque Isle, like the Bonanza on North Main Street.
Phone numbers:	Reach the Bigrock ski area at (207) 425–6711, or in Maine at (888) 592–7625. The number for Aroostook County Tourism is (888) 216–2463.

The International Appalachian Trail, IAT for short, is an approximately 400-mile continuation of the famed Appalachian Trail, running from Georgia to Maine. The Maine section runs from Mount Katahdin to the border crossing with New Brunswick, Canada, at Fort Fairfield, before winding its way deep into Quebec and the Gaspe Peninsula.

To snowshoe a 7.0-mile section of this trail from Mars Hill to the Canadian border at Easton (Maine) and the River de Chute is to walk the line between two countries. A 2.0-mile section of the trail, dubbed the Border Trail, is the defining boundary between the United States and Canada. From the top of the north end of Mars Hill, you can see as far as Katahdin on one side and into the rippling hills, fields, and valleys of Canada on the other. Throw in a rolling ridge line through hardwoods, and you've got an adventure.

Which way to go? That's a question still up for grabs. There are those who suggest starting at the U.S. Customs side for a gradual rise over six 6.5 miles or so to Mars Hill with glorious views and a fast descent down. This might better suit snowshoers who are less sure. The other school gets the steepest part over with at the onset and then enjoys the rolling terrain to the border. For those backcountry skiers looking for a new thrill, the top of Mars Hill to Knoxford Road might be just the thing. Though not skied for this book, ski tracks were spotted on the trail. This appears to be a trail for the more advanced skiers with metal edges. Also, beginner snowshoers can just do the trek along the 2.0-mile Border Trail. Park at the end of Knoxford Road for an access point. Part of this trek does involve walking on a backcountry road.

Directions at a glance

0.0 Leave the Bigrock Ski Area via the Bunny Hill.

0.1 Turn right on connector trail to Ho Chi Minh Ski Trail.

0.6 Reach saddle between north and south peak. Turn left for IAT and soon pass chair lift. (Option exists to turn right for short climb to north peak and lean-to.)

2.7 Reach overlook on north ridge of Mars Hill

4.4 Turn right on Knoxford Road.

5.1 Turn left on International Boundary.

7.2 Turn left at U.S. Customs office on River de Chute Road.

Mars Hill is one of the most notable landmarks in the sparse mountain ranges of Aroostook County. The monadnock leaves the farm land and stands tall at 1,600 feet. There is a ski area along one side of it, Bigrock, which has a rolling 3.5-mile cross-country ski loop. From the top of the north end of Mars Hill, which has a lean-to (bring a tarp to block

A lean-to on the top of the north end of Mars Hill is a fine trip unto itself and a good resting place for those continuing on the International Appalachian Trail.

out the cold winter winds if you spend the night) and some of the best views in all of the county. It is from the base of the ski area that the snowshoe begins. The trail is identified by blue-and-white markers. There aren't any mileage signs. Because the trail is new, the signs are somewhat sporadic.

The trek begins at the base of the mountain, by the bunny slope, where you find an IAT marker. Keep in mind that for the first 1.0 mile or so, skiers and snowboarders will be coming down the mountain. Be alert and stay to one side.

The trek continues up the slope with markers on the side by the T-bar. At the top of the bunny slope, it bears to the right and continues up the ski hill before darting into the woods. Here, the trail begins a series of steep switchbacks along both sides of the Ho Chi Minh Ski Trail. The IAT first stays on one side of the trail, then crosses it and winds again on the other side. At 0.6 mile, the trail reaches a saddle between the north and south ends with fine vistas. The north end is dominated by communication towers, while the south end has a lean-to with picnic table and toilet. It is but a short climb to the top of the north end via a wide, winding trail. The views are worthwhile. Turn right for that one.

Turn left though to continue the trek to the border. The IAT crosses by the top of the chairlift and reenters the tunnellike hardwood forest en route to the north end. The wide trail follows a rolling ridge line and affords valley views through the leafless trees at times. The trail approaches the towers and parallels utility poles along a service road for a short stretch before a brief ascent at the north end. The trail turns right into the forest and begins to drop along the ridge, winding and slabbing across the hill. At one point, the trail breaks out of the woods briefly for outstanding views on the north ridge of Mars Hill, then continues the descent. The trail skirts by a small brook in a tiny bowl-shaped ravine before dropping down, eventually coming out in a field. Stick to the tree line on the right and follow it to Knoxford Road (no sign). Turn right and walk the road 0.7 miles before it ends at what once was a border station. Turn left and follow the rolling trail; Canada is on one side, and the United States on the other. Boundary markers stick out of the snow. The trail drops down to the border crossing by the River de Chute, where one way leads to Maine and the other to Canada.

How to get there

For the Bigrock Ski Area and Mars Hill, bear right at Route 1A north in the town of Mars Hill. In 0.5 mile, turn right on Boynton Road (following signs to the ski area). In 1.0 mile, turn right at the junction and in 0.1 mile, turn left into the ski area.

For U.S. Customs in Easton, take Route 1A north in Mars Hill 5 miles (Henderson's on the corner) and turn right onto Ladner Road. Follow that 7 miles to the border. Ladner Road becomes River de Chute Road. Get permission from customs official to park. The station is open seven days a week from 8:00 A.M. to 4:00 P.M.

For Knoxford Road access, take Route 1A north in Mars Hill about 1 mile and turn right on East Ridge Road. Follow it until the end.

Appendix

MAINE SKI CENTERS

The following are cross-country skiing areas in Maine:

Bethel Inn and Country Club's
  Nordic Center
P.O. Box 49
Bethel, ME 04217
Phone: (207) 824–6274
E-mail: info@bethelinn.com
Web site: www.bethelinn.com

Birches Touring Center
P.O. Box 81
Rockwood, ME 04478
Phone: (207) 534–7305
E-mail: wwld@aol.com
Web site: www.birches.com

Black Mountain
P.O. Box 239
Rumford, ME 04276
Phone: (207) 364–8977

Carter's Cross-Country Ski Center
Route 26, P.O. Box 710
Oxford, ME 04270
Phone: (207) 539–4848

Carter's Cross-Country Ski Center
786 Intervale Road
Bethel, ME 04217
Phone: (207) 539–4848

Five Fields Farm
Route 107
Bridgton, ME 04009
Phone: (207) 647–2425

Harris Farm XC Ski Center
252 Buzzell Road
Dayton, ME 04005
Phone: (207) 499–2678

Inn at Crab Apple
Route 201
The Forks, ME 04985
Phone: (207) 663–4491
E-mail: crabappl@tdstelme.net
Web site: www.crabappleinc.com

Katahdin Lake Wilderness Camps
P.O. Box 398
Millinocket, ME 04462
Phone: (207) 723–9867

Little Lyford Pond Camps and
  Lodge
P.O. Box 340
Greenville, ME 04441
Phone: (207) 280–0016
E-mail: lyfordcamp@aol.com
Web site: www.midmaine.com/
  ~islander/lyford

Lost Valley Touring Center
P.O. Box 260
Auburn, ME 04210
Phone: (207) 784–1561

Rangeley Municipal Trails
P.O. Box 1070
Town Office
Rangeley, ME 04970
Phone: (207) 864–3326
E-mail: mtlakes@rangeley.org
Web site: www.rangeleymaine.com

Ski-a-Bit
RFD 1, P.O. Box 115
West Buxton, ME 04093
Phone: (207) 929–4824
E-mail: mhujsak@aol.com

Ski Nordic at Saddleback
P.O. Box 490
Rangeley, ME 04970
Phone: (207) 864–5671

Smiling Hill Farm
781 County Road
Westbrook, ME 04092
Phone: (207) 775–4818
E-mail: 102135.2067@com-
    puserve.com
Web site: www.mallofmaine.com/
    smiling.htm

Sugarloaf/USA Outdoor Center
P.O. Box 5000
Carrabassett Valley, ME 04947
Phone: (207) 237–6830
E-mail: outdoor@somtel.com
Web site: www.sugarloaf.com

Sunday River Inn and Cross-
    Country Ski Center
RFD 3, P.O. Box 1688
Newry, ME 04261
Phone: (207) 824–2410
E-mail: srinn@nxi.com
Web site: www.sundayriverinn.com

Titcomb Mountain Ski Touring
    Center
P.O. Box 138
West Farmington, ME 04992
Phone: (207) 778–9031

Troll Valley Cross-Country Center
RR 4, P.O. Box 5215
Farmington, ME 04938
Phone: (207) 778–3656

RESOURCES

The following are helpful organizations and resources for planning snowshoe and cross-country ski outings in Maine:

Acadia National Park
P.O. Box 177
Bar Harbor, ME 04609
Phone: (207) 288–3338
Web site: www.nps.gov/acad

Bar Harbor Chamber of Commerce
P.O. Box 158
Bar Harbor, ME 04609
Phone: (207) 288–5103
E-mail: bhcc@acadia.net
Web site: www.barharborinfo.com

Baxter State Park
64 Balsam Drive
Millinocket, ME 04462
Phone: (207) 723–5140

Bethel Area Chamber of
Commerce
P.O. Box 439
Bethel, ME 04217
Phone: (207) 824–2282
E-mail: bethelcc@nxi.com
Web site: www.bethelmain.com

International Appalachian Trail
Maine Chapter
52 Center Street
Portland, ME 04101
Phone: (207) 774–2458

Katahdin Area Chamber of
Commerce
1029 Central Street
Millinocket, ME 04462
Phone: (207) 723–4443
E-mail: kacc@agate.net
Web site: www.mainerec.com/
millhome.html

Maine Appalachian Trail Club
P.O. Box 283
Augusta, ME 04330
(no phone)

Maine Bureau of Parks and Lands
22 State House Station
Augusta, ME 04333
Phone: (207) 287–3821
Web site: www.state.me.us/doc/
dochome.htm

Maine Nordic Ski Council
P.O. Box 645
Bethel, ME 04217
Phone: (800) SKI–XCME
E-mail info@mnsc.com
Web site: www.mnsc.com

Maine Publicity Bureau
P.O. Box 2300
Hallowell, ME 04347
Phone: (207) 623–0363

The Nature Conservancy
(Maine Chapter)
14 Maine Street, Suite 401
Brunswick, ME 04011
Phone: (207) 729–5181

North Maine Woods
P.O. Box 421
Ashland, ME 04732
Phone: (207) 435–6213

Ski Maine Association
P.O. Box 7566
Portland, ME 04112
Phone: (207) 761–3774
E-mail: info@skimaine.com
Web site: www.skimaine.com

Bibliography

The following books proved to be valuable resources and companions in the field research of this book:

Abrell, Diana. *A Pocket Guide to the Carriage Roads of Acadia National Park* (2nd ed.). Camden, Maine: Down East, 1995.

Appalachian Mountain Club. *AMC Maine Mountain Guide* (7th ed.). Boston: Appalachian Mountain Club, 1993.

Jan M. Collins and Joseph E. McCarthy. *Nature Walks in Southern Maine*, Boston: Appalachian Mountain Club, 1996.

About the Author

Marty Basch is a writer, lecturer, and adventurer who has written widely on outdoor recreational themes. He is the author of five books, including *Winter Trails: Vermont & New Hampshire*. His articles have appeared in numerous publications, such as *The Boston Globe, Ski, Ski Trax, Snowboard Life, The Snowshoer, Adventure Cyclist, Mountain Living,* and *AMC Outdoors,* while his syndicated outdoor adventure column can be found in several New England newspapers.

Basch has won awards from the Associated Press for his radio reporting, and was presented with the Harold Hirsch Award by the North American Snowsports Journalists Association for his ski writing.

In addition to skiing and snowshoeing, Basch is also a long-distance bicyclist. His exploits during a 5,198-mile solo journey from Maine to Alaska were chronicled in his book, *Against the Wind*. A 3,000-mile solo cycling trip near and above the Arctic Circle was chronicled in another book, *Above the Circle*. He has also written a guide to mountain biking and road riding in New Hampshire's White Mountains, *The White Mountain Ride Guide*.

Basch lives in New Hampshire's Mount Washington Valley on the Maine border.

Happy Trails to You

Whether you're an accomplished sportsperson or a weekend recreationalist, The Globe Pequot Press can provide you with all of the information you need to find the perfect trails and lodging.

Ramble down hiking paths, cruise through open fields, and visit ski-touring facilities with these books to guide you on the right path.

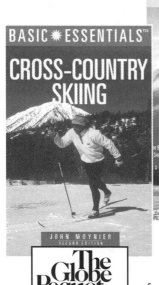

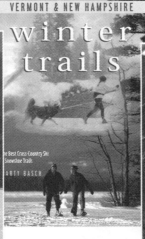

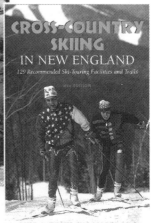